Love Lost
for the Cause of Christ

Love Lost
for the Cause of Christ

*Three Missionaries and Their Sacrifices
for the Great Commission*

WILL BROOKS

WIPF & STOCK · Eugene, Oregon

Wipf & Stock
An Imprint of Wipf and Stock Publishers
199 W. 8th Ave., Suite 3
Eugene, OR 97401

www.wipfandstock.com

PAPERBACK ISBN: 978-1-5326-3559-5
HARDCOVER ISBN: 978-1-5326-3561-8
EBOOK ISBN: 978-1-5326-3560-1

Manufactured in the U.S.A.   07/23/18

For my Hudson, Henry, and Charlotte
May the stories of these three inspire you as they did me

And for Winnie
Who has modeled sacrificial love for me
every day of our lives together

Contents

Acknowledgments

I AM GRATEFUL FOR all the people that helped make this project a reality. I'm thankful to Pickwick Publications for taking a chance on this book. Brian Palmer and RaeAnne Harris have both been very kind and understanding. I've also appreciated the feedback so many colleagues and friends have been willing to give me. One of the many benefits of writing a book like this one is that I've been able to discuss the content of the book with so many people. I've learned so much from others in these discussions – much more than anyone has learned from me.

I could not have completed this book without the help of so many others who were willing to read chapters and provide feedback. Chuck Lawless and I had multiple conversations about the proposal over the course of several years. After all these years of working together, he still helps me to see issues I've overlooked. As usual, Pat Lawson's keen editorial eye helped me refine the writing in several of the chapters. Kyle Faircloth and Phil Barnes also provided much needed editorial feedback. Brian P. and Bo L. both read an early draft of the whole book and did it on short notice. Their feedback helped me recognize that several sections needed significant tweaking.

I am most thankful for my family. My wife was supportive and encouraging throughout this process. Her partnership over the past fourteen years has helped me to understand that the purpose of marriage is for two people to grow together in Christlikeness. I am eternally grateful that God allowed me to share that journey with her. Our three children, each one named after one of the missionaries in this book, have been a constant source of encouragement. My parents also read the entire text and provided much helpful feedback.

Of course nothing is possible in this life apart from God, the giver and sustainer of life. I'm grateful that God has blessed me with so many opportunities and experiences. During some long stretches of my adult life, I often struggled to understand why God had led me where I was at that time. It was only later that I realized God was providing me with the experiences I would not have pursued otherwise. Like so many other things in life, this book is a tribute to his unending faithfulness and lovingkindness. Soli Deo Gloria!

1

Love and the Cause of Christ

THE LIGHTS DIM, THE screen zeroes in on John, and he says to Mary, "It's you. It's always been you, my one true love." In spite of all the obstacles these two main characters have faced, they have accomplished the impossible and attained the unobtainable—they have found true love.

We are familiar with this kind of scene because one exists in almost every contemporary movie. These scenes fill us with happiness, give us hope, and provide that "warm fuzzy" feeling that people want when watching a good movie. They also reveal the fact that many people today consider finding their one true love as critical to their overall happiness and well-being. "If I can just find Mr. Right," they reason, "then I'll be content." But is this cultural value a biblical one? What does the Bible teach us about how we should approach and think about love?

ONE TRUE LOVE

My wife likes to watch Hallmark movies. The nice thing about these movies is that they are clean and free from any kind of explicit language or sexual activity that is so rampant in many television programs and movies today. The downside to Hallmark movies is that the acting is far from great, and there's almost never any massive explosions, car chases, or kung-fu-like fighting sequences that most of us men like. As unrealistic as it is, I'd much rather have an Avengers-style movie where the heroes are so strong that when they shove their enemy, he flies thirty feet away and crashes into a skyscraper, which then implodes and levels an entire city block. But alas, sometimes I have to let my wife chose the movies.

While Hallmark movies are upbeat and lighthearted, the problem with them—and with all romantic comedies for that matter—is that the whole point of the movie is for two people to fall in love. In these movies, two people meet and initially don't like each other. They are usually forced to spend time together, during which they realize they actually like other. For awhile they don't know what to do about liking each other, but finally they decide to be together. Once they decide they are both in love, the movie abruptly ends.

All of these kinds of movies convey a simple idea—finding Mr. or Mrs. Right is critical to one's happiness in life. We gain the impression that once the main character meets that special someone, everything in his/her life is perfect. The problem is that life simply doesn't work that way. Falling in love and getting married is only the starting point of life together. In these movies, we never see the difficulties of the first year of marriage, the realization that one's spouse really isn't perfect, or the long hours of conversation, tears, and prayers that it takes to overcome these and many other challenges.

The point here is not to dissect what makes a happy marriage or why certain movies don't actually portray real-life events. We simply need to recognize that many people today consider finding the right person as critical to happiness and fulfillment. Once they get married, though, they realize that life is not like the movies, and everything is not perfect, wonderful, and easy.

At the same time, many people have the attitude that if you haven't found that person or aren't looking for that person, something is wrong with you. It's only anecdotal, but after I graduated from college and was still single, our church held a special event with a guest speaker. That night, after the speaker introduced himself, he asked all the single people in the audience to stand. When we all did, he then said, "Take a good look around because these are the only options you have left." Not only was this comment hurtful and mean-spirited, it had absolutely nothing to do with the rest of his message. At the time, I was glad to be single, and I was trying to use that time in my life to grow closer to the Lord. His comments bothered me though, because they called into question the idea that there could be any usefulness to being single. Moreover, I knew the other singles in attendance that night, and I knew that many of them were not content with their singleness. I can only imagine how much the speaker's foolish comments hurt them.

Why would a respected speaker make such comments? Unfortunately, these cultural conceptions of happiness and fulfillment affect those within the church too. I've heard similar stories from my students as well. They are serving the Lord faithfully, and yet because they are single, their churches treat them as if something is wrong with them. Just like the surrounding culture, many people in the church believe that finding love is critical to one's happiness.

In the Bible, though, we see that our joy and satisfaction in life is not dependent on being in love or on finding that special someone. The testimony of Scripture tells us that fulfillment only comes from knowing Christ and walking with Christ, not from finding the perfect spouse. Consider Jesus' own teaching. A man comes to Jesus, desiring to follow him, and then makes a simple plea: "Let me first go and bury my father" (Luke 9:60). We expect Jesus to respond with compassion and sympathy, much like any of us would in that situation. We expect Jesus to say something like, "I'm sorry for your loss. Go home, take some time to grieve, and then come follow me." We expect to find kindness and comfort, and yet, Jesus responds, "Leave the dead to bury their own dead."

And then another man comes with a similar request saying, "I will follow you, Lord, but let me first say farewell to those at my home" (9:61). Seems reasonable, right? If this man is really going to follow Jesus, travel where he goes, and not return home, it makes perfect sense that he would want to go home first and let his family know about his plans. In a day before cell phones and email, we can understand why this man wanted to go home first. Once again, we expect understanding and sympathy from Jesus, but like before he replies somewhat cryptically, "No one who puts his hand to the plow and looks back is fit for the kingdom of God" (9:62).

Like all the Gospel writers, Luke liked to string together stories and teachings of Jesus that had similar themes. So if we take a step back and look at the broader context, we see that this is a section of the Gospel where Luke is defining who Jesus is and what it means to be his follower. It starts in 9:18 when Jesus asks his disciples, "Who do the crowds say that I am?" They answer, and then Jesus follows up with a second question, "Who do *you* say that I am?" (emphasis mine). Just like the disciples had to think about this question and decide how to respond, Luke wants his readers to be thinking about how *they* would respond to this question. And his hope is that they would respond the same way that Peter did: "the Christ of God" (9:20).

Peter's response is more than just some kind of head knowledge, but a kind of knowledge that affects how Peter lives. And that's what Luke hopes we see in the following sections. It is for this reason that, right after this interchange, Jesus tells his disciples, "If anyone would come after me, let him deny himself and take up his cross daily and follow me" (9:23). Anyone that desires to follow Jesus must count the cost. We must consider the question, "What if following Jesus means that I lose everything this world has to offer?"

This section of Luke's Gospel gets to the heart of what it means to be a disciple, and discipleship requires followership. Peter and the other disciples believe that Jesus is the Christ of God; they willingly choose to stay with him, and they listen to him. Their choice to follow him is simultaneously a decision to turn their backs on everything the world can offer them.

It is for this reason that Luke includes these difficult sayings of Jesus in this section of the Gospel. He hopes that, as readers reflect on the question of who they say that Jesus is, they will see that a decision to follow him is not a decision made lightly. It is a decision that carries some expectations with it. In other words, a decision to follow Jesus is a decision to deny ourselves and to turn away from all our earthly desires. Not always, but sometimes following Jesus will mean turning our back on family. Not always, but sometimes following Jesus will mean that we give up what others expect us to enjoy—what everyone else in our lives thinks is good, right, comfortable, or easy.

And that includes earthly love. Contemporary culture says that finding love is critical to one's long term happiness. A simple google search will reveal tens of millions of hits and thousands of articles and resources to help one find his/her true love. Some people have even conducted research to determine the odds of finding one's soul mate on any given day, and by the way it's 1 in 562![1] While it's natural to long for companionship in life, Scripture never promises that earthly relationships will satisfy or fulfill us. In fact, the Bible teaches the opposite. The Bible teaches us we will only be satisfied in earthly relationships if we are first satisfied in God.

When someone chooses to follow Christ, Scripture is clear that Christ is to be first and foremost in every aspect of their lives. Ultimate fulfillment and purpose in life comes from knowing him and having a relationship with him. This kind of discipleship, though, often requires us to make decisions between what is good and what is best.

What does this kind of discipleship look like? It's impossible to speak to every situation, but in Matthew's Gospel, he gives us a picture that helps define it. In Matthew 13:44, Jesus uses a parable to illustrate the value and worth of the kingdom of God over against the things of this world. In the parable, a man discovers a hidden treasure in a field, and Jesus explains, "Then, in his joy, he goes and sells all that he has and buys that field." It is fascinating that the man is joyful even though he has to sell everything he owns. Why is he joyful? He is joyful because he recognizes that the treasure in the field is more valuable than everything else he owns.

1. Riley, "What Are the Odds," para. 8.

He gladly gives up all he has so that he can get the field—and of course, its buried treasure.

Becoming a disciple of Jesus means seeing his glory, recognizing that he is more valuable than anything in this world, and choosing to embrace him, no matter the cost. We must see the glory of the kingdom and stand in awe of the majesty of the one who sits on the throne. We see Jesus, love him, find our joy in him, and gladly choose him over all that the world can offer us. In 2 Corinthians, Paul described this process as a light shining into our darkened hearts. What kind of light? It is the light of the knowledge of the glory of God in the face of Jesus Christ. We look to Jesus, and in him we grow in the knowledge of God's glorious nature, his beauty, majesty, and all-surpassing worth. This light shines on us and in us and before us, leading us to a new way of living that glorifies him and says to the world around us, "He is most precious to me."

So it is worth pausing to consider how many of us have lives that resemble the man in Matthew 13. How many of us would gladly give up everything we own if all we got in return was Jesus? We can be thankful that not many of us will be in the kind of situation where our lives depend on how we answer that question. Certainly many places around the world do exist where life and death hinges on how someone answers that question. Though in the West most of us may not lose our lives when we confess faith in Christ, and we often don't have to sacrifice or give up much when we become believers, it is helpful to think about the question. In fact, one could make the argument that's it critical to ask ourselves this kind of question, because if we don't, we could be in danger of loving this world and the benefits and pleasures of this world more than we love Christ.

Of course, this process of loving Christ more than the world doesn't happen overnight, and it doesn't happen easily. That's why Jesus emphasized that his disciples must learn to carry their cross *daily*. It's a process that takes a lifetime, and one in which we progress slowly. Personally, one of the things the Lord has used in my life to encourage me in this process is the testimonies of other saints. It's kind of like in Hebrews 12, where after recounting all the amazing acts of faith of former saints in Hebrews 11, the author writes, "since we are surrounded by so great a cloud of witnesses, let us . . ." His statement helps us to understand that he has included this chapter because he wants us to emulate their example by living by faith, looking to Jesus, and awaiting his return. God often uses the testimonies of others to encourage us and challenge us to cherish Christ more completely and run our race more faithfully.

Just today I was with some of my students who are from a place where it's not always easy to be a believer. They told me that before they became believers, and especially when they made the decision to enter into full time ministry, they had to consider the question I mentioned above, what if going into the ministry means losing everything else? Since there are not many male believers in some of their hometowns, a couple of the ladies mentioned that they realized that entering into full time ministry probably meant that they would never get married. Listening to their testimonies and the way they chose to cherish Christ and labor for him no matter the cost encouraged me to love and serve him more faithfully.

God often uses the testimonies of others to encourage and challenge us, and many times those testimonies are of saints who have long gone on to be with the Lord. Although they lived at different times and in different contexts than us, we can often relate to the challenges they faced. The ways that they trusted in the Lord, depending on his power and expecting his provision encourage us to do the same in our day and time.

In this book my goal is to focus in on missions history and consider how missionaries have often made tremendous sacrifices for the sake of the gospel. In missions history, we examine how the church has sent the gospel out from one cultural context and sought to implant it in a different one. Doing so has never been easy and it has never been done without sacrifice. So we might ask the question, why were these men and women motivated to leave home, travel to faraway places, learn new languages, study culture, and embrace suffering?

It is staggering to consider the fact that throughout church history millions of believers have been burdened by the fact the church does not exist in other parts of the world. They have looked at maps and realized that there are other countries, cities, people groups, villages, and tribes, all of which have no access to the gospel. This knowledge has led them to weep and pray and strategize, and ultimately to send people out from their churches—God-called, Sprit-empowered, Jesus-exalting people who would go to these locations and peoples for the sake of the gospel. Take a minute and stop to think about how amazing that fact is. In church history, millions of people have been willing to leave behind everything they had ever known, in many cases the only place they had ever lived, to go to places where they had never been and in which they knew not even one person. Why? What could possibly motivate them to do such a strange thing? Their sole motivation was that they loved Jesus Christ and longed for him to be known and worshipped.

Considering the fact that in some way, shape, or form all missionaries have had to make certain kinds of sacrifices, my goal is to zero in on one specific type of sacrifice, namely earthy love. In other words, this study started with the question of whether or not there were missionaries who chose to lay aside earthly love for the sake of serving Christ. Are there stories of people who were in love or who were engaged, then felt God's call to take the gospel to the nations, and were willing to sacrifice the prospect of earthly love in order to obey God's call on their life?

We have already seen how contemporary culture values finding true love. Therefore if we could identify a few people from past generations who were willing to sacrifice earthly love and happiness for the sake of obeying God's call, it might help us to understand that faithfulness to Christ is more important than earthly happiness.

FOR THE LOVE OF CHRIST

Numerous examples exist in church history of people who loved Christ more than this world. In this book, though, we want to focus in on three of those people. These three people willingly, gladly, and joyfully sacrificed earthly love. Given that we've already seen how much contemporary culture values finding Mr./Mrs. Right, the testimonies of those in the book will seem strange to many. Many Christians probably won't even understand why these three made the decisions that they did. Those decisions will only make sense if we first understand that it was love for Christ that led them to make these sacrifices.

In chapter two, we will consider the life and testimony of Henry Martyn. To many from our day and time, his life will seem like a massive waste. A brilliant scholar who graduated at the top of his class, Martyn could have done anything he wanted. What he wanted, though, was to follow God's call to the nations. He was burdened for the people of India who had no access to the gospel. His health was weak and his family and friends warned him that life in India would not be easy. He went anyway, devoting his time and energy to translating the Scriptures into as many dialects as possible.

We will see that before leaving for India, Martyn fell in love with Lydia Grenfell. To Martyn, Lydia was perfect in every way imaginable, except one—she did not share his burden for India. Martyn did all he could to convince her to change her mind. In the end, he had to make a choice. Would he choose earthly happiness with the one he loved, or would choose obedience to the call of God?

In the next chapter we'll meet Lottie Moon. Like Martyn, Moon also showed exceptional academic ability in her youth. At a time when education for women was a new idea in the South, she had the dream of opening and running her own school. She eventually achieved that dream, but in the process, she became burdened for the lost in Japan and China. She laid that dream aside for a bigger dream—bringing the gospel to the millions in China who had no access to it. For much of her life, she lived alone in isolated areas so that the people she loved might have an opportunity to hear the gospel in their lifetime. She also wrote numerous letters back to the United States, pleading for churches to send out more people to join her.

During at least one point in her life, she too was in love. Her letters show that she planned to leave China, move back to the United States, and get married. Had she done so, her story could've had the makings of a modern day romantic movie. The one she loved was her former professor, though they'd lost contact for many years. One in the United States and one in China, they were reunited by several friends and began writing to each other. We can almost see the modern day movie title, "Their Love Crossed Oceans." For Moon, though, this story was not the one her life would tell.

The fourth chapter will tell the story of Hudson Taylor. The most well known of these three, Taylor knew that he was called to China at a young age. As a result, he spent most of his teenage years preparing for that work. His early years in China were difficult, living through a civil war, often having little money to survive on, and dealing with long periods of loneliness. Younger than most other missionaries, Taylor began to spend all of his time with the Chinese. He also found it was easier to blend in when he wore the same types of clothes as them. Eventually, he would start his own mission sending organization that adopted many of the principles that he learned during those early years.

Taylor's story is a bit unique in that he did get married. Before getting married, though, he was engaged once and nearly engaged a second time. Both times the women were in love with him but not in love with the idea of living in China. Taylor was forced to make a choice—a wife or China? These two sacrifices were not the only ones that Taylor made in regards to love. We will see that after falling in love with someone who shared his passion for the work, God would call him to sacrifice her as well.

In the final chapter, we will tie all of these themes together. Considering the missionaries and the sacrifices they made for the cause of Christ, how then should we live today? What sort of sacrifices should we be willing to make? How can we seek to be more faithful to Christ and to his Great Commission? In other words, our goal is to examine how we might follow the example of these three missionary heroes by living lives of unyielding faith and by being willing to sacrifice every possible worldly comfort on the altar of Christ. In sum, we will be encouraged to live for one thing—to see Christ exalted and enjoyed in the darkest parts of this world.

As we begin this study, let me also admit my bias. As one who has lived overseas for a significant amount of my adult life and who has lived and worked and traveled in many of the places that these missionaries lived, I have tremendous respect for who they were and what they did. They are my heroes. I remember the first time I read a biography on Henry Martyn. In my mind I can still see myself sitting in my living room, wiping away tears as I read about the pain and sickness Martyn experienced in India. Oh how the Lord has used their stories to challenge and inspire me to greater faithfulness. It is my prayer that he would use the recounting of their testimonies here to do the same for you. And with that prayer in mind, we turn our attention to Henry Martyn.

QUESTIONS FOR CONSIDERATION

1. How does contemporary culture celebrate the idea of finding true love? Can you think of other examples of this cultural value?

2. How do the difficult sayings of Jesus in the Gospel of Luke help us to understand the high cost of discipleship?

3. What does it mean for a disciple to carry his cross daily? How have you seen this teaching fleshed out in your own life?

4. What if following Jesus meant having to give up every other good thing in your life? Would you still follow him?

5. What does Scripture teach about true contentment and fulfillment? How does biblical teaching contrast contemporary cultural ideals?

I have not felt such heart-rending pain since I parted with Lydia in Cornwall. But the Lord brought me to consider the folly and wickedness of all this. I could not help saying, "Go, Hindus, go on in your misery, let Satan still reign over you; for he that was appointed to labor among you is consulting his ease." No, thought I, earth and hell shall never keep me back from my work.

—Henry Martyn

He went forth to preach the gospel to the lost, and it was his fixed resolution to live and die amongst them. When he left England, he left it wholly for Christ's sake, and he left it forever.

—John Sargent, on Martyn's commitment

2

Love Postponed: Henry Martyn

IMAGINE TRANSLATING THE FIRST half of Isaiah 1:18, "Though your sins are like scarlet, they shall be as white as snow," into a language that has no word for snow because the people have never before seen it. Or how about translating the second half of the same verse, "Though they are red like crimson, they shall become like wool," into a language that doesn't distinguish between red and crimson, or one that doesn't have a word for wool because there are no sheep where that language is spoken. It makes my brain hurt just thinking about it! There's no doubt that one of the most important (and difficult!) tasks in missions is the translation of the Scriptures.

In all of church history, perhaps no one has excelled at this task more than Henry Martyn. Martyn was only on the mission field for six short years, but he was a burning flame whose life left a lasting legacy. In that short time, Martyn translated the New Testament into Urdu and Persian, the Psalms into Persian, and he also worked on an Arabic translation of the New Testament. He was a genius who harnessed all his gifts and abilities to exalt Christ in one of the spiritually darkest parts of the world, and he made enormous sacrifices along the way. In this chapter, we'll examine his life and consider one of the most significant sacrifices he made in order to follow Christ's call to the nations.

HIS LIFE AND WORK

Salvation and Calling

Henry Martyn was born on February 18, 1781 in Truro, England. The early years of his life saw much change. England lost the American colonies in 1781; they observed the French Revolution with horror when it began in 1789; and even in Martyn's own hometown, coal miners were forced to confront armed soldiers during a demonstration because of low wages and inhumane working conditions.[1] The church likewise saw change when, in 1792, William Carey sailed to India and became known as the Father of the modern missions movement. Carey's example challenged evangelicals in England and the New World to take the gospel to the ends of the earth.

William Carey's work would influence Martyn, but in his youth, he was uninterested in religion and was focused solely on academics. As a child, he excelled in courses like Greek and Latin, despite the fact he gave almost no effort to memorization. His teacher remarked that it was "as if he learned it by intuition."[2] When Martyn finally began to apply himself, his genius was evident to all. In 1801, while studying at Cambridge, he won the top award in the school for Mathematics, and the next year, while focusing almost solely on Mathematics, he won an award for Latin.

During those years of academic success, Martyn's older sister would often speak to him of Christ. He once wrote, "The sound of the gospel, conveyed in the admonition of a sister, was grating to my ears."[3] All that would change in 1800, though, when Martyn's father suddenly and unexpectedly passed away. Martyn understood the fleeting nature of life and the vanity of all the world has to offer. While studying astrology, he came to the conclusion that far more important than the study of the stars themselves was the

---

1. Cromarty, *For the Love of India*, 23.
2. Sargent, *Life and Letters*, 3.
3. Sargent, *Life and Letters*, 8.

study of the Maker of the stars. At this realization, he gave his life to Christ.

Later that year, Martyn stood for an examination, which was the culmination of his years of study at Cambridge. When the school published the results, he discovered that he had taken first prize. After winning the Mathematics award he had worked so hard for, one would think Martyn would be ecstatic. Since trusting in Christ, though, his perspective had changed. While reflecting on his accomplishment, he wrote, "I obtained my highest wishes, but was surprised to find that I had grasped a shadow."[4]

A key component of Martyn's post-conversion life was his commitment to the local church.[5] His pastor in Cambridge, Charles Simeon, was a man who faithfully preached the word of God, and his teaching helped Martyn grow in his understanding of the things of God. On one occasion in 1802, while teaching a Bible study on missions, Simeon mentioned the impact of William Carey's work in India.[6] Having seen the emptiness of worldly pursuits, Martyn was gripped by the example of William Carey—he wanted his own life to have the same kind of eternal impact that Carey's was having in India. God had called Henry Martyn to India.

Embracing such a call was not easy or without pain. Martyn's biographer explains,

> Nor let it be conceived that he could adopt this resolution without the severest conflict in his mind, for he was endued with the truest sensibility of heart, and was susceptible of the warmest and tenderest attachments. . . . How then could it fail of being a moment of extreme anguish when he came to the deliberate resolution of leaving forever all held dear upon earth? But he was fully satisfied that the glory of that Savior who loved him, and gave Himself for him, would be promoted by his going forth to preach to the heathen; he considered their pitiable and perilous condition; he thought of the value of their immortal souls. . . . Actuated by these motives, he offered

4. Sargent, *Life and Letters*, 15.
5. Sargent, *Life and Letters*, 14.
6. Sargent, *Life and Letters*, 22; Cromarty, *For the Love of India*, 51.

himself in the capacity of a Missionary to the Society for Missions to Africa and the East; and from that time stood prepared, with a child-like simplicity of spirit, and an unshaken constancy of soul, to go to any part of the world, whither it might be deemed expedient to send him.[7]

Martyn would spend the next three years preparing for missionary service, but during that time he faced significant opposition from friends and family. Martyn's family had a history of lung-related illnesses (no one in his family lived past thirty-five years old), so many of his friends didn't think his body was healthy enough for a life in India. His sister didn't think he was experienced enough. After pouring out his heart for two hours to one friend about God's calling, that friend responded by saying that Martyn had neither the body nor the mind to become a missionary.[8]

Now, just for a second, put yourself in Martyn's shoes. Have you ever experienced something similar? Has there ever been a time when God called you to do something or to go somewhere, but all those around you thought it was a bad idea? We can easily imagine the internal struggle that Martyn faced during this period in his life. He was excited about God's call and his new purpose in life, but he found no enthusiasm and little support from those closest to him. How would he respond? Would he abandon his calling and follow the advice of others? How would you respond?

For Martyn, all that mattered was God's will. He wrote in his journal, "What am I that I should *dare* to do my own will."[9] His friend and biographer John Sargent wrote of his resolve, "But he was fully satisfied that the glory of that Savior who loved him, and gave Himself for him, would be promoted by his going forth to preach to the heathen."[10]

He also grew in holiness during those days. He wrote of being "permitted" to do God's will, recognized how unworthy he was to

7. Sargent, *Life and Letters*, 25–26.
8. Smith, *Henry Martyn*, loc. 444.
9. Sargent, *Life and Letters*, 35.
10. Sargent, *Life and Letters*, 25–26.

have been called to such a monumental task.[11] Later he wrote, "May it be sweet to me to proclaim to sinners like myself the blessed efficacy of my Savior's blood! May He make me faithful unto death! The greatest enemy I dread is the pride of my own heart."[12] When a new year began in 1803, he examined his life and found that in the previous year he had spent too much time in aimless pursuits and too little time in the pursuit of God.[13] He wrote:

> My soul approves thoroughly the life of God, and my one
> only desire is to be entirely devoted to Him; and oh may
> I live very near to Him in the ensuing year, and follow
> the steps of Christ and his holy saints. I have resigned,
> in profession, the riches, the honours, and the comforts
> of this world; and I think also it is a resignation of the
> heart.[14]

Martyn didn't concern himself with whether or not his experience was thorough enough, if his mind was sharp enough, or if his body was strong enough. The important thing was that God had called him. He wrote on those days, "My thoughts were full of what God will do for his own glory."[15] He continued, "I did not wish to think about myself in any respect, but found it a precious privilege to stand by, a silent admirer of God's doings."[16]

India and Persia

Today, traveling from London to Calcutta might take twelve hours, but in 1805 it took Henry Martyn eight months to complete the journey. It's no wonder why, in Martyn's day, no such thing as short-term missions existed! In those days, ships first sailed to San Salvador on the east coast of South America, then to the Cape of

11. Sargent, *Life and Letters*, 43.
12. Sargent, *Life and Letters*, 44.
13. Sargent, *Life and Letters*, 50.
14. Sargent, *Life and Letters*, 50–51
15. Sargent, *Life and Letters*, 79.
16. Sargent, *Life and Letters*.

Good Hope in South Africa, and then to India. Martyn used the time to preach to the others on the ship, to study Hindu, and to strengthen his already granite-like resolve. John Sargent explained Martyn's conviction during this season of his life, "When he left England, he left it wholly for Christ's sake, and he left it forever."[17]

During a stopover in San Salvador, Martyn had the opportunity to speak with a Catholic, a Muslim, and an atheist all in one day. In his journal he recorded his thoughts: "I never felt so strongly what a nothing I am. All my clear arguments are good for nothing: unless the Lord stretch out his hand, I speak to stones. I felt, however, no way discouraged; but only saw the necessity of dependence on God."[18] He also struggled with loneliness writing,

> Whilst sitting to rest myself towards night, I began to reflect, with death-like despondency, on my friendless condition. Not that I wanted any of the comforts of life, but I wanted those kind of friends who loved me, and in whose company I used to find such delight after my fatigues. And then, remembering that I should never see them more, I felt one of those keen pangs of misery that occasionally shoot across my breast. It seemed like a dream—that I had actually undergone banishment from them for life; or rather like a dream, that I had ever hoped to share the enjoyments of social life. But at this time I solemnly renewed my self-dedication to God; praying that I might receive grace to spend my days in his service, in continued suffering, and separation from all I held dear in this life. Amen. How vain and transitory are those pleasures which the worldliness of my heart will ever be magnifying into real good! The rest of the evening, I felt weaned from the world and all its concerns, with somewhat of a melancholy tranquility.[19]

When Martyn finally arrived in India he felt overwhelmed, burdened by the multitudes who needed to hear the gospel. In his journal, Martyn wrote that while still in England, he had imagined

17. Sargent, *Life and Letters*, 91.

18. Sargent, *Life and Letters*, 123.

19. Sargent, *Life and Letters*, 137–38.

that upon arriving in India he would immediately lead many to Christ. Standing on Indian soil, though, the task seemed much more challenging. He wrote that he needed a strong faith to support the "apparent impossibility"[20] of his converting anyone. Nonetheless, arriving in India was a solemn event. He wrote, "Now that I am actually treading on Indian ground, let me bless and adore my God, for doing so much for me; and Oh, if I live, let me have come hither for some purpose."[21] He committed himself to the task and penned the words, "Now let me burn out for God."[22]

During those early days in India, he recognized God's sovereign hand guiding him. He also saw that the results he desired were ultimately not dependent upon him:

> Walked by moonlight, reflecting on the Mission. My soul was at first sore tried by desponding thoughts; but God wonderfully assisted me to trust him for the wisdom of his dispensations. . . . How easy for God to do it; and it shall be done in good time: and even if I never should see a native converted, God may design by my patience and continuance in the work to encourage future missionaries.[23]

Martyn spent the next five years in India doing three primary tasks: starting local schools, preaching the gospel, and translating the Scriptures. On one typical day, his journal describes dealing with animism and idolatry when sharing with a Hindu, debating the Quran while sharing with a Muslim, fulfilling administrative responsibilities at a school he started, and spending an evening translating the Bible into a local dialect.[24] He gave himself little rest, waking early and often staying up late into the evening wrestling with the best way to translate a passage of Scripture into the

20. Sargent, *Life and Letters*, 146.
21. Sargent, *Life and Letters*, 144.
22. Smith, *Henry Martyn*, loc. 1815.
23. Sargent, *Life and Letters*, 146.
24. Rhea, *Life of Henry Martyn*, loc. 214.

local language.[25] Unfortunately, his body could not keep up with his relentless work ethic.

Despite frequently suffering from chest pains, he would preach four times on Sunday, writing that it took him until Tuesday to fully recover from the effort.[26] Already weak from his respiratory issues, the heat sapped what little strength remained. A coworker explained Martyn's state after traveling by horse in extreme heat:

> Thus, Mr. Martyn travelled, journeying night and day, and arrived at Cawnpore in such a state, that he fainted away as soon as he entered the house. When we charged him with the rashness of hazarding his life in this manner, he always pleaded his anxiety to get to the great work. He remained with us ten days, suffering considerably, at times, from fever and pain in the chest.[27]

Martyn simply would not allow himself to rest while there was so much left to do for Christ's sake. He wrote in his journal:

> Come what will, let me only be found in my path of duty, and nothing shall be wrong. Be my sufferings what they may, they cannot equal those of my Lord, nor, probably, even those of the apostles and early martyrs.[28]

The task Henry Martyn loved more than any other was Bible translation. He began translating the New Testament book of Acts into Urdu and Persian after only six months in India.[29] After eleven months, he had finished translating a number of parables and written commentary on them.[30] At fourteen months, he finished translating Acts into Urdu.[31] By twenty-four months, he had

---

25. Sargent, *Life and Letters*, 220.

26. Rhea, *Life of Henry Martyn*, loc. 252.

27. Sargent, *Life and Letters*, 260.

28. Sargent, *Life and Letters*, 179.

29. Sargent, *Life and Letters*, 161.

30. Sargent, *Life and Letters*, 199.

31. Sargent, *Life and Letters*, 214.

finished the Urdu New Testament,[32] and by thirty-four months, he had translated all four gospels into Persian.[33] What he accomplished in such a short time is breathtaking—that he did it while busy with so many other tasks is utterly mind-boggling.

He loved the Bible and longed for the lost around him to have an opportunity to read it: "O how refreshing and supporting to my soul was *the holiness of the word of God*; sweeter than the sweetest promise, at this time, was the constant and manifest tendency of the Word, to lead men to holiness and the deepest seriousness."[34] Later he explained his relentless work ethic writing, "What a wretched life shall I lead, if I do not exert myself from morning till night in a place, where, through whole territories, I seem to be the only light."[35] And later after spending a day translating the parables, he wrote, "My soul much impressed with the immeasurable importance of my work, and the wickedness and cruelty of wasting a moment, when so many nations are, as it were, waiting while I do my work."[36]

In 1811, after five years in India, a translation committee evaluated the translations that Martyn and his coworker Sabat had been working on. They praised Martyn's Urdu translation, but found his Persian and Arabic translations lacking in quality. Given that Martyn was translating into a language that wasn't widely spoken where he was living, it is no surprise that the committee found the translations of little value. The committee's comments helped Martyn to see that he must move to Persia, and then hopefully to Arabia to complete these two translations.

Leaving India was another solemn event for Martyn. He wrote on that day:

> I now pass from India to Arabia, not knowing the things
> that shall befall me there, but assured that an ever-faithful
> God and Savior will be with me in all places withersoever

32. Sargent, *Life and Letters*, 237.

33. Sargent, *Life and Letters*, 256.

34. Sargent, *Life and Letters*, 168.

35. Sargent, *Life and Letters*, 178.

36. Sargent, *Life and Letters*, 182.

I go. May He guide and protect me, and after prospering me in the thing whereunto I go, bring me back again to my delightful work in India! I am perhaps leaving it to see it no more; but the will of God be done; my times are in his hand, and He will cut them as short as shall be most for my good: and with this assurance, I feel that nothing need interrupt my work or my peace.[37]

Once in Persia (modern day Iran), Martyn dedicated the bulk of his time to his translation, but he also engaged local religious leaders in numerous debates. While these Muslim leaders attacked the Christian understanding of Jesus as God's Son, Martyn wrote, "The more they wish me to give up this one point, the Divinity of Christ, the more I seem to feel the necessity of it, and rejoice and glory in it. Indeed, I trust I would sooner give up my life than surrender it."[38] On one occasion, after completing his translation and having it printed, he hoped to present a copy to the king. A mob began to angrily question him about Jesus, and, fearing for his life (and for the beautifully printed copy of his translation), he carefully wrapped up the Bible and fled. In his journal, he reflected on the events, "What have I done, thought I, to merit all this scorn? Nothing I trust, but bearing testimony to Jesus."[39]

While he was living in Shiraz, Persia, the locals often ridiculed and maligned Martyn. He wrote, "Their sneers are more difficult to bear than the brickbats which the boys sometimes throw at me."[40] We see Martyn's godly character in that he went on to say, though, that he considered persecution for Christ "an honor of which I am not worthy."[41] Every time others would persecute him, he would pray: "If on my face for Thy dear name, shame and reproaches be; All hail, reproach, and welcome, shame, if Thou remember me."[42]

37. Sargent, *Life and Letters*, 278.
38. Sargent, *Life and Letters*, 321
39. Sargent, *Life and Letters*, 368.
40. Sargent, *Life and Letters*, 321.
41. Sargent, *Life and Letters*.
42. Sargent, *Life and Letters*.

Having finished his Persian New Testament, and, with his health once again in decline, Martyn decided to return to England for rest and recovery. He hired a guide, who provided horses, and together they charted a course through Turkey. Unsympathetic to Martyn's failing health, the guide rode hard through long days in extreme heat. With a bad cough, probably pneumonia, and high fever, Martyn would collapse at the end of each day's ride and beg to rest the next day—until one day he never woke up. Henry Martyn died at age thirty-one in Tocat, Turkey on October 16, 1812.

LOVE POSTPONED

Martyn made the ultimate sacrifice, giving up his life for Christ, but his death was not the only sacrifice he made in order to do God's will. Shortly before leaving England, Martyn met Lydia Grenfell and immediately fell in love with her. From that point forward, his life was consumed with thoughts of her. Day after day, he recorded in his journal how he was wrestling with and discussing with others the prospect of marrying Lydia before going to India.[43] And day after day his attitude seemed to change as to whether marriage or singleness was God's will for him.

In June 1805, only a few months before Martyn would sail to India, he found his "affections kindling"[44] to the idea of marriage. Just a few days after that journal entry, though, he wrote that the idea of marriage had become an idol to him and that the thought of being with Lydia had become a temptation for him to abandon his calling.

Perhaps you can relate to Martyn's predicament. How was he to understand these new desires of his heart? Just a few months earlier, his situation seemed so simple—God had commanded him to go and go he would. But now, he had to determine if he was to go alone, or if he should first pursue marriage. How was he to

43. Smith, *Henry Martyn*, loc. 724.
44. Smith, *Henry Martyn*, loc. 699.

understand God's will? It is easy to understand why his journal records an almost daily flip-flopping on his perspective.

As Martyn wrestled with what to do, his response ultimately came down to a single question: Would he seek his own comfort, or would he obey Christ's command? In his journal he recorded his answer, "I could not help saying, 'Go, Hindus, go on in your misery, let Satan still reign over you; for he that was appointed to labor among you is consulting his ease.' No, thought I, earth and hell shall never keep me back from my work."[45]

Roughly one month later, when his ship's departure was delayed, Martyn had one final opportunity to visit Lydia. He wrote of that morning, "With much confusion I declared my affection for her, with the intention of learning whether, if ever I saw it right in India to be married, she would come out."[46] Lydia responded that she needed time to think about his proposal—it was certainly not what Martyn was hoping to hear. Even though the response was not what he had hoped, Martyn would remain devoted to Lydia Grenfell for the rest of his life.

In his conversations with friends, his journals, and his letters, Henry Martyn made his feelings for Lydia clear. Her feelings for him, however, are a bit of an unknown. On the day that Matryn declared his affection, Lydia wrote in her journal that she hoped her response made it clear he was free to marry someone else and that she would pray for him to find a "suitable partner."[47] At the same time, though, she wrote of the anguish and conflict she experienced at seeing Martyn leave. She likewise wrote that she tried to conceal her true feelings from him, fearing that he might abandon God's call to stay with her.[48]

When it was finally time to leave for India, Martyn experienced tremendous pain and heartache. Though he was obeying God's call, leaving Lydia behind was the hardest thing he had ever

45. Sargent, *Life and Letters*, 86.

46. Smith, *Henry Martyn*, loc. 972.

47. Smith, *Henry Martyn*, loc. 1107.

48. Smith, *Henry Martyn*.

done. He wrote in his journal of his "heart-rending pain"[49] and "extreme anguish,"[50] explaining, "My heart was sometimes ready to break with agony."[51] Faced with the depths of despair, Martyn threw himself toward God, the fountainhead of true and unending joy. He found comfort in the hymn, "The God of Abraham I praise," which states, "I all on earth forsake; Its wisdom, fame, and power; And Him my only portion make; My shield and tower."[52] Martyn had truly forsaken all—giving up that earthly thing which was most desirable and most precious, because in the end, God was his only portion. Obedience to Christ was more important than life or love or any other thing.

Henry Martyn had left Lydia behind and set his heart toward India, but he certainly had not forgotten her. As he traveled, his thoughts frequently turned to her. During a brief stopover at the Cape of Good Hope, Martyn wrote in his journal, "In my walk home by the sea-side, I sighed on thinking of Lydia, with whom I had stood on the shore before coming away, and of the long seas that were rolling between us."[53] Though there was pain in leaving and pain in separation, God gave him a sense of peace. Above all else, Martyn knew that God had ordained his circumstances for his good, and as a result, he maintained a devotion to "no object upon earth but the work of Christ."[54]

After being in India for a year, though, his coworkers and friends from England convinced him to revisit the idea of marriage. The effectiveness of his work faced significant obstacles in his current isolation, frequent loneliness, and weak health. A wife, though, would remedy all of these weaknesses, while supporting him in advancing the kingdom for years to come.[55] Convinced marriage to Lydia was the will of God, Martyn sat down to write.

49. Sargent, *Life and Letters*, 86.
50. Sargent, *Life and Letters*, 93.
51. Sargent, *Life and Letters*, 86.
52. Sargent, *Life and Letters*, 92.
53. Sargent, *Life and Letters*, 136.
54. Sargent, *Life and Letters*, 416.
55. Sargent, *Life and Letters*, 228, 417.

In the letter, Martyn explained how he had come to this decision, and he wrote that his primary motivation in seeking marriage was the advance of God's kingdom in his own heart and among the lost. He told Lydia that if their marriage would not help him in his pursuit of God and serve to promote the gospel, "May God in his mercy withhold it."[56]

Now consider our own generation and the expectations we have concerning how quickly others should respond to us. We send a text, and we expect an immediate response. We send an email, and we get impatient if a full day passes without a response. Now, there's no doubt that given the magnitude of the question he'd just asked, Martyn wanted to hear back from Lydia as quickly as possible. Since communication between India and England was so slow at that time, though, he would have to wait fifteen months to receive her response![57]

When Martyn finally received Lydia's response, she had rejected his proposal. It did not help that only a short time earlier he had received the heartbreaking news of his sister's death. Dejected and suffering, Martyn penned a prayer in his journal that her rejection would help him to love the things of the world no longer. He wrote, "With Thee, O my God, is no disappointment. I shall never have to regret that I have loved Thee too well."[58] Martyn would not be denied so easily, and he immediately set about writing Lydia another letter, one in which he sought to persuade her and respond to her possible objections.[59]

Lydia never accepted his proposals and would never join him in India. They would continue to write to one another, and Martyn undoubtedly thought of her often. Before leaving for Persia, he recorded in his journal:

> Was walking with Lydia; both much affected, and speaking of the things dearest to us both. I awoke, and behold, it was a dream! My mind remained very solemn and

56. Sargent, *Life and Letters*, 418.
57. Sargent, *Life and Letters*, 425–26.
58. Sargent, *Life and Letters*, 228.
59. Sargent, *Life and Letters*, 425–31.

pensive; I shed tears. The clock struck three, and the moon was riding near her highest noon; all was silence and solemnity; and I though with pain of the sixteen thousand miles between us. But good is the will of the Lord, even if I see her no more.[60]

Later he wrote to her saying, "Five long years have passed, and I am still faithful."[61] Since leaving England, his love for Lydia had not wavered.

As his time in India came to an end and he sailed to Persia to perfect his Persian and Arabic translations, he pondered a possible return to England. In a letter written around this time, Lydia mentioned that a return to England was his duty. He responded by saying that her duty was "not to let me come away again without you."[62]

Two years later when his Persian translation was finished, he began the long trip back to England, and as sickness began to overtake him, his thoughts once again turned to Lydia. In fact, the last time his pen ever touched paper was to write her a letter.[63] In that letter he wrote, "Soon we shall have occasion for pen and ink no more; but I trust I shall shortly see thee face to face."[64] Martyn never stopped hoping that he could persuade Lydia to marry him and join him in his work of taking Christ to the nations.

Today, more than two hundred years after his passing, Henry Martyn's missionary legacy lives on not only because of what he accomplished but also because of what he sacrificed. His genius in Bible translation staggers us. His relentless effort for the cause of Christ challenges us. His willingness to expose his weak body to so many dangers and so many illnesses inspires us. And of course, his decision to leave Lydia, in a sense postponing love until he could convince her to join him, exhilarates us and emboldens us to likewise choose Christ over all the world has to offer.

60. Sargent, *Life and Letters*, 272.
61. Sargent, *Life and Letters*, 437.
62. Sargent, *Life and Letters*, 440.
63. Rhea, *Life of Henry Martyn*, loc. 86.
64. Sargent, *Life and Letters*, 463.

In the end, his life came down to one question: what was most precious to him? Was it academic achievement or academic reputation? He was certainly close to his sisters and his other friends. Were those relationships the most enjoyable thing in his life? Or how about Lydia, the love of his life? Was her companionship most precious to him? If he had stayed in England, he most certainly could have spent more time with her, and likely even married her. For Henry Martyn, though, all this was loss compared to the "surpassing worth of knowing Christ Jesus" (Phil 3:8). For him, there was one great passion, one great purpose—to cherish Christ above all things and make him known in the darkest parts of this world.

QUESTIONS FOR CONSIDERATION

1. What aspect of Henry Martyn's story inspired you the most?

2. After winning the mathematics award at Cambridge, Martyn said he felt like he had "grasped a shadow," because the achievement was not as satisfying as he imagined it would be. Have you ever felt that way? How do worldly accomplishments compare with knowing Christ?

3. What's the relationship between missions and the Bible? In other words, why was it important for Henry Martyn to devote so much time to Bible translation?

4. Martyn wrote that he maintained a devotion to "no object upon earth but the work of Christ." How did such a devotion affect his relationship with Lydia? Is it right for us to maintain such a devotion?

O, that I could consecrate myself, soul and body, to his service forever; O, that I could give myself up to him, so as never more to attempt to be my own or to have any will or affection improper for those conformed to him.

—Lottie Moon

3

Love Surrendered: Lottie Moon

ONE OF THE MOST controversial questions in missions is related to the role of women, especially single women. During the so-called Great Century (1792–1910) of missions advance, many women were simply considered missionary wives, and their commitment and calling to the work was not even evaluated before they were sent out. Her husband was the missionary, and she was simply accompanying him. In a later chapter, we'll see that the organization Hudson Taylor started, China Inland Mission, changed this approach because they recognized that both husband and wife must be prepared to endure the challenges of life on the field. Moreover, because they were sending missionaries to places where the gospel had never gone before, both husband and wife needed to be equipped to advance the gospel in those areas.

China Inland Mission, like other organizations of their day, also began sending single women to the field. This may not seem so controversial in our day, but it certainly was in the late nineteenth century. And once mission organizations began to practice this, it opened up a host of other controversial questions—for example, what kind of work should they be involved in? Is it safe to send them to cities or villages where they will be on their own? Should they share the gospel with men, or should they only preach to women? And then what happens once they start a church—if they won't preach to or disciple men, how will they adequately train leaders for this new church?

Even today, no easy answers exist to these questions, and to be fair, these questions exist because, in the history of missions, women have been much more willing to embrace the hardships of missionary life. In 2009, one Southern Baptist leader lamented that, of the fifty single missionaries the denomination had sent to West Africa, forty-eight of those were women.[1] His point was not to decry the critical role that women have played or continue to play in missions today, but simply to ponder this question: "Where are all the men?" For her part, in a different time and a different context, Lottie Moon asked the same question. In this chapter, we will consider her life, calling, work, and perhaps most importantly for our purposes, the life she sacrificed to obey God's call.

LIFE AND WORK

Salvation and Calling

Charlotte Digges Moon was born in 1840 in Albermarle County near Charlottesville, VA. Her grandfather was the largest land-owner and slaveholder in that county. After his death, his children divided up the land and separated the slaves. It is interesting to note that, for a time, Moon's uncle owned Monticello, the former home of Thomas Jefferson. After corresponding with Karl Güt-zlaff, whose writings also influenced Hudson Taylor, he sold Monticello and decided to become a missionary to China.[2] His mother, though, not only forbid his leaving, but persuaded him to stay by giving him several houses and enough money to open his own pharmacy. After his mother's death, he became the first Disciples of Christ missionary to Jerusalem, and even wrote a book about archaeological discoveries in Israel.[3]

---

1. Akin, "Word From Paul," 8.

2. Allen, *New Lottie Moon*, 16–19; and Sullivan, *Lottie Moon*, 23.

3. Barclay, *Jerusalem As It Was*.

Moon was the fourth child in her family, and her father died when she was only thirteen. Contrary to many of his day, Moon's father saw the value of education for females, and thus he encouraged and enabled his daughters to pursue their academic goals. Moon's older sister Orianna became the first woman from Virginia and only the second in the South to gain a medical degree. Moon herself had tutors until she was old enough to attend a boarding school. When she graduated from Hollins Academy at the age of sixteen, she was already one of the most educated women in Virginia. At that time, though, more institutions were beginning to see the value of women's education, and some Baptist leaders decided to open the Albemarle Female Institute in Charlottesville, VA. Moon was in the second class admitted to the school.

While at Albemarle, Moon developed a reputation for two things: her intellect and her mischievousness. She was the top student in the school in languages. By the time of her graduation, she had become proficient in Greek, Latin, Italian, French, and Spanish, and the faculty had even given her special approval to study Hebrew.[4] Her Latin exam was so impressive that her professor recommended that the entire faculty review it. When reviewing her moral philosophy exam, Professor Hart wrote to John Broadus to explain that it was the best he had ever seen.[5] She finished the normal three-year course of study and stayed for a fourth. Moon and four others completed so many hours by the end of the four years that the trustees awarded them the Master of Arts degree. They were the first women in the South to earn such a degree.[6] In fact, at the time of her graduation, John Broadus wrote that she was the most educated woman in the South.

While no one doubted Moon's intellect at Albemarle, it might be surprising for some to find out that she was not very religious. In her first year at Albemarle, other classmates considered her a troublemaker. At the time, even though their mother was a devout Baptist, older sister Orianna was an atheist and "took pride in her

4. Allen, *New Lottie Moon*, 38–39.
5. Allen, *New Lottie Moon*.
6. Allen, *New Lottie Moon*, 39.

lack of religion."[7] It seems that Moon desired to follow her sister's example more than her mother's. In fact, she was not only uninterested in religious things, but she actively ridiculed those who so passively accepted their parent's religion without any study or investigation of their own. On one occasion, a student asked what her middle initial "D" stood for, and she responded "Devil." At the time, no one could have imagined that in the years to come Moon would almost daily be reviled on the streets in China as a "foreign devil," a term she loathed and sought to confront whenever she heard it used.

Many of Moon's classmates considered her lost and often prayed for her. Julia Toy, sister of Crawford Toy (whom Moon considered marrying at least once in life) pleaded with Moon to consider God's grace in her life and trust in Christ.[8] In December 1858, John Broadus held an evangelistic meeting, and for weeks in advance students prayed for unsaved classmates, including Moon.[9] On the night before the meeting, Moon was unable to sleep because of a barking dog, and she lay in bed all night considering the state of her soul. The next night, she attended the meeting and had a long conversation afterward with Broadus. She decided to give Christianity an honest investigation. A few weeks later, she confessed her faith in Christ. As Regina Sullivan explains, "Moon's own conversion came not in an emotional evangelical convulsion but rather through a rational decision to open her mind to a new intellectual pursuit."[10]

And pursue she did. From that point forward in her life, she devoted all her intellectual prowess toward knowing God and making him known. Her classmate Julia Toy explained, "She has always wielded an influence because of her intellectual power. Now her great talent was directed into another channel."[11] Another classmate stated that it seemed Moon was "God's chosen vessel. In

7. Sullivan, *Lottie Moon*, 21.
8. Allen, *New Lottie Moon*, 34–35.
9. Allen, *New Lottie Moon*, 35.
10. Sullivan, *Lottie Moon*, 25.
11. Allen, *New Lottie Moon*, 35.

his own time, he brought her to his feet, meek, submissive, ready to do any work the master assigned."[12]

Some of Moon's classmates never finished their studies because their parents considered marriage more important than graduation. And in the pre-Civil War South, people rarely entered into marriage out of love but more often did so based on financial considerations. Moon's biographer Catherine Allen notes that since Moon's father had already passed away and since her family was financially stable, no one put pressure on her to leave school and marry.[13] Moreover, she considered what God might be calling her to do in the future. Her pastor John Broadus kept the students aware of the lost around the world. He directed these calls for gospel laborers to the male students and to the female students only as potential missionary wives. Lottie Moon, though, wasn't interested in being a missionary wife. She wanted to be a missionary, regardless of whether or not she had a husband.

At that point in time, though, Southern Baptists were not sending single females to the mission field, which has led some people to assume that Moon had intentions to marry.[14] It was during her time at Albemarle that Moon first met Crawford Toy, who was her professor for English and Greek. Many students developed crushes on Professor Toy, and while Moon and Toy stayed in contact for years after her graduation and were romantically involved later in life, no evidence exists that they were interested in one another at this point in time. That said, Toy and another young man John Johnson (who was engaged to Julia Toy, Moon's friend and Crawford Toy's sister) both made a commitment to foreign missions and the Foreign Mission Board of the Southern Baptist Convention appointed both to be missionaries.[15] They planned to sail in the fall of 1860, but Johnson became ill, and he and his wife could not make it to the ship in time. Toy never explained his

12. Allen, *New Lottie Moon*.

13. Allen, *New Lottie Moon*, 38.

14. Moon's first biographer, Una Roberts Lawrence, makes this assumption (Lawrence, *Lottie Moon*, 92).

15. The information in this paragraph is from Allen, *New Lottie Moon*, 37.

absence from the ship, but some scholars have assumed that he decided to wait until he could find a wife to travel with him.[16]

After that sailing in the fall of 1860, Southern Baptists didn't send anyone to the mission field for some time. By the time of Moon's graduation in the spring of 1861, South Carolina had already seceded from the Union, and only one month later the first major battle of the Civil War was fought at Bull Run in Manassas, VA, about one hundred miles away from Moon's home. For someone like Lottie Moon who had grown up in a wealthy, slaveholding holding family in the South, the war disrupted and altered the life she had always known. It also affected her future employment possibilities.

During the war, Moon's older sister Orianna served as a surgeon, and in the early stages of the war, Moon served as her secretary, corresponding with others on her behalf. During this time a potential suitor came to their home to call on Moon. That suitor eventually served as a military chaplain, but after staying at the Moon home for a few days, he left, "without Lottie's promise of undying love."[17] In the later stages of the war, Moon worked as a tutor in Georgia, South Carolina, and Alabama.

When the war ended in 1865, the Moon family finances were in shambles. Moon's own finances were one-fortieth of what they were before the war.[18] Moreover, a real fear existed that the Northern army would ride through and ravage what had been left untouched during the war, especially since the war ended so close to the Moon family plantation. When news of the war's ending reached Viewmont, Moon's mother told her to bury many of the family's valuables for safekeeping.[19] The act was done in such haste, though, that when it became clear that army wasn't coming, the family was unable to relocate the valuables.

Given the family's post war financial situation, Moon needed work, and she found it as a teacher at a girls' school in Danville,

16. Allen, *New Lottie Moon*.
17. Allen, *New Lottie Moon*, 46.
18. Allen, *New Lottie Moon*, 55.
19. Allen, *New Lottie Moon*, 48–49.

KY. Kentucky was a border state during the war, and thus, it citizens fought on both sides of the Civil War. From a historical perspective, it is interesting to note that both Abraham Lincoln and Confederate President Jefferson Davis were born in Kentucky. Since it was a border state, though, it received financial support from the Union Army throughout the war, and thus, its financial situation was much better after the war than any southern state. Perhaps this was one of the reasons Moon looked for employment there as opposed to somewhere closer to home.

Moon taught in Kentucky for four years and then relocated to Cartersville, GA to run a newly opened school for girls. Through-out her time in KY and in GA, Moon's desire to become a mission-ary only grew stronger. What was surprising to her was that, when her mother died in 1870 and she returned to VA, she found out that her younger sister Edmonia (Eddie) had also experienced a call to missions and desired to go to China. At the time, Southern Baptists were not sending single females as missionaries, but the post-Civil War environment had forced them to rethink the issue of women's roles in the church. With more women working out of financial necessity, it was only natural that many would start ask-ing, "If I can work in the secular world, why can't I do more in the church?"[20] Moon herself published an article on the topic in which she posed a series of similar questions:

> There is a latent power in our churches, which follow-ing the wise example of other denominations, we should seek at once to develop. . . . These [women] could make it their business to minister to the poor and suffering, establish Sunday school, sewing schools, night schools, and mothers' meetings. In a large city, such an instru-mentality would be invaluable in reaching the poor, the degraded, and the ignorant. Scores never enter a church for want of clothing. . . . How are such people to be reached, then? Evidently the gospel message must be carried to their homes, and actual trial has shown that women are peculiarly fitted for just this kind of work. Our Lord does not call on women to preach, or to pray

20. Sullivan, *Lottie Moon*, 33.

in public, but no less does he say to them than to men, 'Go, work today in my vineyard.' Does anyone object that women cannot be found to devote themselves to this work? All history refutes this imputation on women's readiness for self-consecration.[21]

While these discussions were ongoing, the Foreign Mission Board hired Henry Tupper as the Corresponding Secretary (President in modern terminology) in 1872, and Tupper was open to the idea of sending single females as missionaries. Eddie had already been writing on a regular basis to Southern Baptist missionaries in China, and she and Moon were contributing forty-five dollars per year to support their work there. Upon Tupper's appointment as Secretary, Eddie immediately began corresponding with him, and the Board appointed her as a missionary to China that same year.

Moon began to correspond with Tupper in 1873. When Eddie arrived in China, Moon wrote to her to inquire of the longer serving missionaries about the need for single females in that part of China. One of those missionaries then wrote to Tupper explaining that Moon was a potential candidate. Upon hearing of his letter, Moon wrote to Tupper to explain that she was under several obligations that prevented her from going, and thus, she didn't want the letter to be made public. Not only was she under contract at the school in GA, but she had also agreed to care for a relative's children in the case of death. She wrote that she had considered before of offering herself as a candidate but these obligations prevented her from doing so, and she was considering seeking a release from them.[22]

In February of 1873, Moon's pastor preached a sermon on missions, and she told him that his sermon "cemented" her decision to leave for China.[23] In July of that year, the Foreign Mission Board appointed Lottie Moon as a missionary to China. She would sail just a few months later, but before leaving she published an article that was in perfect harmony with the legacy she would

21. Sullivan, *Lottie Moon.*
22. Harper, *Send the Light,* 4.
23. Allen, *New Lottie Moon,* 68–69.

eventually leave for Southern Baptists. In that article, she pleaded with others—men and women—to join her on the great endeavor of taking the gospel to the nations:

> Young brethren, can you, knowing the loud call for la-
> borers in the foreign field, will you settle down with your
> home pastorates? So many could be found to fill your
> places at home; so few volunteer for the foreign work. For
> women, too, foreign missions open a new and enlarged
> sphere of labor and furnish opportunities for good which
> angels might almost envy. . . . Could a Christian woman
> possibly desire higher honor than to be permitted to go
> from house to house and tell of a savior to those who
> have never heard his name? We could not conceive a
> life which would more thoroughly satisfy the mind and
> heart of a true follower of the Lord Jesus.[24]

China

In 1873, it took Lottie Moon nearly two months of travel to get from the United States to her destination in China. She was on a ship for twenty-five days in transit from San Francisco to Yokohma, Japan, during which time she was continually seasick. After spending some time in Yokohama and Nagasaki, she boarded another boat bound for Shanghai, but they encountered a typhoon and had to return. When she finally made it to Shanghai, she needed to wait for several coworkers to conduct business before they could accompany her back to Shandong province, where she would spend most of the next forty years of her life.

It didn't take long for Moon to recognize the needs in her new place of service. After being on the field for about a week, she wrote to Tupper stating, "At our very doors is the work we crave." Then she went on to describe how those who had no knowledge of Christ were "literally all around us" and how in some places "the women crowded eagerly to hear the words of life."[25] How

24. Allen, *New Lottie Moon*, 71.
25. Harper, *Send the Light*, 5.

did she respond to these needs? While some would have been overwhelmed, she threw herself into the work and pleaded for more help. In that same letter to Tupper she wrote, "What we need in China is more workers."[26]

For the rest of her life she would not stop pleading for reinforcements. In 1874 she wrote a journal article in which she described traveling out to the country to share the gospel in several villages. She wrote in that article of "the Lord's call for men to labor as evangelists among these villages. It is said that in three years' time one could hardly visit them all, so numerous are they."[27] She wrote to Tupper describing the openness to the gospel and stated, "Oh! That we had many active and zealous men who would go far and wide scattering books and tracts and preaching the Word to the vast multitudes of this land."[28] And after another trip to the countryside, she asked Tupper to speak to Southern Baptists for her saying, "We implore you to send us help. Let not these heathen sink down into eternal death without one opportunity to hear that blessed gospel which is to you the source of all joy and comfort."[29]

Back in the United States, many in her denomination were debating women's roles in the church and on the mission field. For Moon, though, these were not theoretical discussions. While most Christians in her day believed that women should not engage in preaching and teaching, Moon wrestled with the fact that she was surrounded by so many men for whom there was no male witness. What should she do? If she chose not to share the gospel with them, she would effectively condemn them to an eternity in hell since she might be the only witness they would have in this lifetime. On the other hand, if she chose to share with them, her own denomination might condemn her and consider her a heretic.

---

26. Harper, *Send the Light*, 6.

27. Harper, *Send the Light*, 175.

28. Harper, *Send the Light*, 8.

29. Harper, *Send the Light*, 17. At the time, "heathen" was a word used to describe non-Christians. In time, Moon realized that the term was derogatory toward those she was trying to reach and she stopped using it.

This inner struggle is one of the reasons she was so adamant that the Board send more men to the field.

After she began to gain language proficiency, Moon began traveling to the countryside with Sally Holmes, a fellow missionary who would become her mentor. Before Moon arrived on the field, a gang with an anti-foreigner mentality murdered Holmes' husband. Holmes, pregnant at the time and having only been on the field for one year, stayed in China, gave birth to a son, and continued the work. On one occasion while traveling with Holmes, Moon feared others might think she crossed the line of appropriate work for women. She wrote home to Tupper, "I hope you won't think me desperately unfeminine, but I spoke to them all, men women [and] children, pleading with them to turn from their idolatry to the true and living God. I should not dared to remain silent with so many souls before me sunk in heathen darkness."[30]

It didn't take Moon long after arriving on the field to realize that her sister Eddie was not well. Eddie mastered the language quickly, but she seems to have experienced severe culture shock. A number of issues contributed to her condition, and before long, the mental stress of cross-cultural living began to affect her health. In 1876, after Moon had been on the field for three years, she and others encouraged Eddie to take a short break from her work. Eddie traveled with a few others to Nagasaki, but unfortunately her condition only worsened on the journey. Her companions wrote to Moon encouraging her to come to Nagasaki immediately, and when she arrived she decided that Eddie needed to return to the United States at once.

Moon accompanied Eddie back to Virginia. Once she returned, though, she found out that the Board didn't have the money to send her back to the field. During her time in the United States she was able to meet with Tupper, who wrote of their meeting, "It was good to be in the company with one who feels specially called to labor among the far-off heathen, and who, after experiences of its hardships and difficulties, returns to her work, not merely with cheerfulness, but with a spirit of quiet Christian

---

30. Harper, *Send the Light*, 32.

exultation."[31] When some Baptist women raised money for Moon to build a house in China, she asked that she be able to use some of the money to pay for her return trip. So in November of 1877, one year after returning to VA, Lottie Moon sailed to China for a second time.

Moon had always dreamed of opening a school for girls in China, and upon her return she did just that. That work was not without difficulties. To a missions society in Georgia she explained that Chinese typically did not educate women and did not see the value in it.[32] As a result, it was difficult for her to recruit students. Many Chinese recognized that the worldview of the missionaries was at odds with their own and thus, did not want to send their sons or daughters to such a school. It didn't help that the treaties that enabled missionaries to live in China grew out of the imperialist desires of the Western world and were forced upon the Chinese government.

It is easy to criticize the strategies used by missionaries in the past, especially when so many in the nineteenth century conducted their work with attitudes of Western superiority. In those days missionaries often used words like "heathen" or "uncivilized" to describe the people they were trying to reach, and their strategies often failed to distinguish biblical truth from cultural tendencies. Lottie Moon was not immune to these failures. It is fascinating to read that after several years on the field, she still didn't like Chinese food and still had not mastered using chopsticks.

That said, the longer she stayed on the field, the more Moon grew in this area. More and more, she was traveling with Sally Holmes out to the countryside for evangelistic work. She wrote to Tupper that in one village she was so exhausted, she decided she would do no more work that day. Almost immediately after she made that decision though, the people crowded around her and it was "impossible to keep silence."[33] She went on to say, "We have 'the words of eternal life' [and] we *must* speak them to this people

31. Allen, *New Lottie Moon*, 113.

32. Harper, *Send the Light*, 181.

33. Harper, *Send the Light*, 79.

in spite of all weariness."[34] In a later letter she described the joy she felt in these events:

> Is it any wonder that as you draw near to the villages a feeling of exultation comes over you? That your heart goes up to God in glad thanksgiving that he has so trusted you as to commit to your hands this glorious gospel that you may convey its blessings to those who still sit in darkness? When the heart is full of such joy, it is no effort to speak to the people: you could not keep silent if you would. Mere physical hardships sink into merited insignificance. What does one care for comfortless inns, hard beds, hard fare, when all around is a world of joy and glory and beauty?[35]

These countryside experiences helped her to make the decision to abandon her work with the school in order to embrace a more evangelistic strategy in a smaller city where Southern Baptists had no other missionaries. She wrote to Tupper explaining, "*Under no circumstances do I wish to continue in school work.* I confess it would please my ambition to build up a big school, but I long to go out [and] talk to the thousands of women around me. . . . If I am to devote myself to evangelistic work in the city [and] country, I *must* be free from the school."[36] Moon loved teaching and educating, but her heart beat for those who had no access to the gospel.

In one article she wrote for Southern Baptists back in America, she described what it was like to live in a place with no believers on a Sunday morning:

> If there is anything calculated to make one feel the fact of being in a heathen land, it is to pass through the streets on the Sabbath. Stepping out of your street door, on your way to church, you find yourself at once in the middle of a busy throng. Perhaps it is market day, and the streets are lined on either side with bags of grain, donkeys, mules, and men. A busy traffic is going on. Everywhere, as you

---

34. Harper, *Send the Light*, 80.
35. Harper, *Send the Light*, 89.
36. Harper, *Send the Light*, 102–3.

proceed on your way, are evidence of a land without a Sabbath. Hawkers vend their wares, peddlers call attention to their goods, children play about the streets, men gossip or discuss business—the busy tide of life rolls on. Probably not one in all that vast throng is aware that it is the Lord's holy day. How you long to see this thoughtless, careless, busy multitude, winding its way to the house of God![37]

While Moon longed for many Chinese to come to the knowledge of Christ, she learned to be patient since the harvest was slow to come. She explained:

One should not be discouraged by the extremely slow progress of the gospel in the heathen lands. To be impatient of early results is as if pioneers, in an unbroken wilderness, with forests to be cut down, houses to be built, lands to be cleared, the soil to be plowed and sown, should be dissatisfied that houses do not grow up by magic, nor broad acres, in a moment, wave with golden harvests. The hearty pioneer plods on patiently, year after year, and in time he reaps the reward of his labor. So in heathen lands, we must wait patiently during the time of seed-sowing. The harvest will come in time, and in China what a harvest it will be![38]

Sixteen years after she accompanied Eddie back to the United States, Lottie Moon took a second furlough from her work. The Board had approved her furlough some time earlier and Moon felt that considering her overall health she needed a break from the work. Nonetheless, she wrote to Tupper in the intervening years saying, "I *cannot* leave those eager people without the certainty that others will carry on the work."[39] In that same letter she explained, "I would I had a thousand lives that I might give them to the women of China!"[40]

37. Harper, *Send the Light*, 184.
38. Harper, *Send the Light*, 214.
39. Harper, *Send the Light*, 132.
40. Harper, *Send the Light*.

While continuing to labor alone as a pioneer, she wrote to Southern Baptists pleading for them to send more workers. While many pastors in the United States would have criticized her communicating the gospel to men, she wrote to them stating the facts of her situation:

> How do you mean to remedy this abnormal state of affairs? For three years I have been working, mostly alone, in an interior city called Pingtu. I am expecting to spend the winter there alone. Not only women and girls are asking to be taught, but men are earnestly inquiring the way of life. As I am the only Baptist missionary within one hundred miles, these men must look to me this winter for instruction and guidance. I do not complain of the burden laid upon me by teaching heathen men in addition to my legitimate work among the women and girls. I merely come to you and state the facts.[41]

She then posed a question for these pastors to consider, "What are you going to do, *yourselves in person*?"[42]

Moon would take another furlough in 1904, and at that time many people encouraged her to retire. She responded, "Oh, don't say that you don't want me to return. Nothing could make me stay. China is my joy and my delight. It is my home now."[43] She returned to China for another eight years. During those final years, living in the countryside area became too difficult so Moon resumed her educational work, starting a school for boys and one for girls. She wrote that she primarily taught them from the New Testament and that she experienced such joy in seeing them grown not only in knowledge but also in character.[44]

After nearly forty years of ministry in China, Lottie Moon died in 1912 in the harbor of Kobe, Japan, while traveling back to the United States due to ill health. Moon's first biographer explained that in the midst of a famine in Shandong and either out

---

41. Allen, *New Lottie Moon*, 179–80.

42. Allen, *New Lottie Moon*.

43. Allen, *New Lottie Moon*, 238.

44. Harper, *Send the Light*, 338–39.

of a self-sacrificial love for the Chinese people or as a protest to the FMBs continuing financial problems and lack of monetary support to alleviate suffering in that region, Moon refused to eat until those around her ate first. As a result, she starved herself to death before her coworkers could get her the medical attention she needed.

A recent work has challenged this explanation and concluded that Moon actually developed dementia in the fall of 1912.[45] While that explanation is most likely true, we should not attribute any ill motives to Moon's first biographer. Few people in the early twentieth century recognized or were able to diagnose dementia. Her coworkers recognized that something was wrong, writing that Moon was not eating and that she seemed to be acting strange.[46] When they made plans to help her return to the United States, then Secretary of the FMB Willingham wrote that "her mind has become impaired" and that she was suffering from "nervous trouble."[47] Before making it back, though, a coworker traveling with her wrote, "She steadily became weaker until her poor tired suffering body fell asleep and her soul went to be with the Lord."[48]

In the years since her death, her story has motivated Southern Baptists to obey the Lord's Great Commission more faithfully. The yearly Christmas Offering named for her is the single most important offering each year for international missions among Southern Baptists. Nonetheless, Keith Harper aptly explains:

> She literally gave her life in service to her God and deserves to be remembered as more than a mere symbol. Moon's life and work are urgent reminders that while missionary work seeks to bring the Divine to humanity, it is nonetheless a very "human" endeavor. Missionaries attempt to touch people as individuals rather than pursue statistical glory. Moon learned this lesson by living, and ultimately dying, among the people she wanted to

45. Sullivan, *Lottie Moon*, 5–8, 155–59, 152.

46. Harper, *Send the Light*, 446–47; 450.

47. Harper, *Send the Light*, 448–49.

48. Harper, *Send the Light*, 451.

reach. May her legacy outstrip superficial symbols and be one of loving commitment to her God and the people she felt called to serve.[49]

LOVE SURRENDERED

Moon labored in China for nearly forty years, and while she had numerous coworkers and companions throughout that time, she lived a large portion of it alone. In a time period when women were primarily seen as homemakers, she was highly educated and chose her own vocation. Even in missions where most people saw women primarily as companions or "missionary wives," she served as an evangelist in a pioneer area, bringing the gospel to those who formerly had no access to the gospel.

Though she never married, Moon was not without love in her life. We already mentioned the possibility that a chaplain visited her home during the early stages of the Civil War hoping to win her affection. Not much is known about this story except that it didn't work out. Far more important to Moon was her relationship with Crawford Toy. Toy had been her professor at Albemarle Female Institute, and the Foreign Mission Board had appointed him as a missionary to Japan. For some unknown reason, he never sailed to Japan and some scholars have assumed that he was waiting until he found a wife. After the Civil War, he went to Germany to study theology and Semitic languages. In 1869 he returned to the United States and began teaching at Southern Seminary, which had moved to Louisville, KY after the Civil War ended.

It is difficult to reconstruct the relationship between Moon and Toy since no letters between the two still exist today. When Toy started teaching at Southern Seminary in Louisville though, Moon was about eighty miles away in Danville, KY. It is possible that the two rekindled their friendship at that time, as a letter exists from Moon to her mother that alludes to a love interest at that

---

49. Harper, *Send the Light*, 445.

time.[50] Whatever communication or interest they had in one another at that time faded as Moon moved to GA. Two years later the FMB appointed her as a missionary and she left for China. Moon chose to obey the call of God rather than pursue the possibility of marriage.

Fast forward three years when Moon accompanied Eddie back to the United States because of her health issues and ultimate resignation from the FMB. Once again it is difficult to know why or how, but it seems that the correspondence between Moon and Toy resumed at this time. Catherine Allen wrote that Tupper and President of SBTS John Broadus encouraged Toy to visit her while recruiting for the school in VA.[51] Regardless of how their friendship was rekindled, what is clear is that after Moon returned to China, Toy began to advocate for female missions in China and even helped to start several women's missions organizations in KY.[52]

Not only had Moon encouraged Toy to become an advocate for missions in China, but Toy was also influencing Moon. In her letters to Tupper she began using a new phonetic that was invented by Toy. She wrote, "I hav adopted the fonetic style of spelling, but I shal not dare to spel that way if your compositor snubs me by putting my letters in type in the old way. Plese let me kno."[53] In a following letter she wrote, "Don't yu admir the nü speling?" Not long after, though, she reverted to the traditional writing style.

Toy had been at Southern Seminary for almost ten years, but during that time it became evident that his time in Germany had influenced him toward views that were not in line with the doctrinal statements of Southern Seminary and the denomination as a whole. Toy resigned from Southern and in 1880 took a position teaching at Harvard. In the aftermath of these events, the FMB appointed two men as missionaries to China, but later, when finding

50. Sullivan, *Lottie Moon*, 55.
51. Allen, *New Lottie Moon*, 112.
52. Sullivan, *Lottie Moon*, 55.
53. Harper, *Send the Light*, 92.

out that they had studied under Toy and accepted his views, re-
scinded their appointment.

In spite of these developments, Tupper wrote to Moon and
spoke positively about Toy. She responded, "I trust he has a bright
future before him at Harvard."[54] Their relationship continued to
strengthen. Sullivan states that Moon's letters from these years dis-
play a loneliness and increasing ambivalence toward the work.[55]
Perhaps she experienced these feelings because Eddie was no longer with her, or perhaps they grew out of the fact that despite her
constant pleas, Southern Baptists were not supporting the work in
the ways she felt like they needed to. Conflict between missionaries also created additional pressure, and Moon often acted as a
mediator.[56] In fact, ten years later in 1893, these conflicts became
so great that Moon asked to be reassigned to Japan.[57] Whatever the
reason, it is clear that Moon was considering leaving the field and
marrying Toy.

In 1881, the mission in Shandong was in a difficult situation. Several missionaries were returning to the United States and
Moon's mentor, Sally Holmes, had recently retired, leaving only
Moon and one other. The missionaries met to discuss the future
of the mission, and in that meeting Moon announced to the group
that she would be leaving the field to become Toy's wife and teach at
Harvard.[58] Harvard, though, would not have female professors for
another forty years so it possible that Moon misunderstood Toy or
that Toy had overpromised. Either way, Moon wrote to her family
to prepare for a spring wedding. The wedding was even announced
in the Kentucky and Mississippi state Baptist newspapers.[59]

---

54. Harper, *Send the Light*, 97.

55. Sullivan, *Lottie Moon*, 54.

56. For a description of the Crawford-Hartwell feud that threatened to
destroy the Shandong mission, see Sullivan, *Lottie Moon*, 42–48.

57. Harper, *Send the Light*, 150–51.

58. Allen, *New Lottie Moon*, 138.

59. Sullivan, *Lottie Moon*, 56.

Moon's original biographer wrote that Moon and Toy planned to marry and then return to the field as missionaries.[60] This plan seems unlikely, though, since the FMB had decided not to send the two men who had adopted Toy's theological views. After that decision, it is difficult to imagine how Moon could think they the FMB would send Toy himself. It is far more likely that due to loneliness and frustration with the work, Moon was considering leaving the field, marrying Toy, and relocating to Harvard.

As we know from her biography, Moon never followed through with this decision. The wedding never happened. Some scholars have concluded that Moon changed her mind after a thorough examination of Toy's theological views. In fact, Allen explains that Toy's family understood that the engagement was broken off due to religious differences, and she wrote that some later missionaries noticed a number of books in her library related to the Toy controversy.[61] At the time she wrote to her family about a wedding, though, she was already well acquainted with Toy's views and had been in contact with him for several years so this reasoning seems unlikely.

Since a two year gap exists in the communication between Moon and Tupper and since no letters between Moon and Toy still exist, it is impossible to determine exactly why they never married. A statement that Moon made later in life, though, seems to shed some light on her decision-making process. A young relative asked Aunt Lottie if she had ever been in love. Moon replied, "Yes, but God had first claim on my life, and since the two conflicted, there could be no question about the result."[62]

In the end it seems most likely that Moon considered her calling and recognized that she did not want to turn her back on the work in China. Though the work was hard, the stresses great, the comfort little, the companions few, and the harvest slow, it was God's work, and for better or worse, she was committed to it. There would be no wavering or turning back. She had committed

---

60. Sullivan, *Lottie Moon*, 55.

61. Allen, *New Lottie Moon*, 138.

62. Allen, *New Lottie Moon*, 139.

herself to this work, and she would not change course now. More-over, with others leaving Shandong, she was the only one left from whom millions of people could hear the gospel message. If she left, what hope did they have? A sense of responsibility and a burden for the lost held her in place even when her heart was leading her elsewhere. The words Moon wrote on the inside cover of her Bible reflect this attitude.

> O, that I could consecrate myself, soul and body, to his service forever; O, that I could give myself up to him, so as never more to attempt to be my own or to have any will or affection improper for those conformed to him.[63]

Lottie Moon's story is one of self-sacrifice, of love for God, and of commitment to his mission over against all the things of this world. She served faithfully for nearly forty years and never stopped encouraging others to join her in this Christ-exalting task. More than once in life she was faced with a crossroads and she had to make a decision. Would she continue pursuing her dream of leading a school for girls in Georgia, or should she obey God's call and go to China? Should she return to China, or stay with her sister Eddie in Virginia? Should she continue educating girls in the city, or should she adopt the hardships of the countryside so that she might have more opportunities to share the gospel?

Of course, her relationship with Toy and plans to marry was another significant turning point. Staying in China would mean embracing loneliness and discomfort and culture shock. Marrying would not only give her companionship but also the comforts and privileges of being married to a Harvard professor (and perhaps one day teaching there herself). As she told her young relative, though, God had first claim on her life. How did she make decisions when she reached these turning points? She trusted him and trusted his plan and his calling. Anything in conflict with that was surely abandoned.

---

63. Allen, *New Lottie Moon*.

QUESTIONS FOR CONSIDERATION

1. Many of Lottie Moon's classmates never finished college because they got married. At a time when very few women worked outside the home, how radical was it for Moon to shun marriage and continue toward a degree? What does this attitude say about her character which would later help her as a missionary?

2. When did Moon first feel burdened for missions? Why did she not then immediately leave for the mission field? How did she use the intervening years? What does her story teach us about the need for patience as we wait for God's plans for us to unfold?

3. What were some of the challenges Moon faced on the mission field? How did she respond to these difficulties?

4. Why did Moon stop teaching for a few years and move to a smaller city? How was this work different from the work she was doing before? What does this action tell us about Moon's primary motivation for being in China?

5. When did Moon first meet Crawford Toy? How did their relationship develop over the years? Why do you think she didn't leave the field to marry him?

6. How does Moon's statement that "God had first claim on my life" affect how we should view marriage, sacrifice, and obedience to the Great Commission?

Not outwardly only but inwardly also he had accepted the will of God, giving up what seemed his best and highest, the love that had become part of his very life, that he might be unhindered in following Christ.

—Howard Taylor

I almost wish I had a hundred bodies; they should all be devoted to my Savior in the missionary cause.

—Hudson Taylor

4

Love Sacrificed: Hudson Taylor

PERHAPS THE MOST CHALLENGING aspect of life as a missionary is learning to function in a different cultural context. People in other cultures don't just speak another language; they also think, act, and communicate in different ways. Such different mentalities can wreak havoc on a person who is used to communicating in one way and then is forced to communicate differently. When I first moved to Asia, my friends kept asking me, "What is your staple food?" I wasn't familiar with the concept of eating the same staple every day. I had no idea how to answer my friends' question. Our miscommunication, though, was not simply the result of language differences. It grew out of our different cultural backgrounds. Our cultures had different ways of *thinking* about food, and thus, these differences limited our ability to communicate.

The church's understanding of how culture affects the missionary task has developed over time. One of the men who has best helped missionaries think about how to live and function and thrive in a different culture is Hudson Taylor. In a time when missionaries were primarily sent from the West to the East, those missionaries often functioned in largely Western ways. They wore Western clothes, built Western-style homes and church buildings, used Western educational methods, passed out Western medicine, and so on. At a time when Western culture was intermingled with the preaching of the gospel, Hudson Taylor was profoundly counter cultural. In fact, he was shunned by most of his missionary colleagues when he adopted Chinese dressing styles. In response to these criticisms, Taylor wrote that he was more than willing to forsake "the company and approval of Westerners in order to gain the friendship and confidence of the Chinese."[1]

Hudson Taylor's story is primarily one of love—love for China and, more importantly, love for Christ. Taylor's desire that the Chinese would come to know the love of Christ drove him to embrace a life of suffering and sacrifice. Of the three missionaries surveyed in this book, Hudson Taylor is the most well-known. Many people are familiar with his adoption of Chinese dress, of his founding of the China Inland Mission, and of his life of faith and dependence on God alone for all his needs. Fewer people are familiar with the fact that, on multiple occasions and in multiple ways, he was willing to sacrifice earthly love for the cause of following Christ. In this chapter, we'll first take a brief look at his life and legacy and then consider the love he sacrificed.

LIFE AND WORK

Salvation and Calling

Hudson Taylor grew up in a Christian home with parents who were very active in their faith. Though his father was not a full-time pastor, he often preached at their church. As he prepared to preach, he and Taylor's mother would study the passage and discuss potential applications together. Not long after they were first married, the Lord impressed upon their hearts the statements in the Old Testament that say, "Sanctify unto me all the firstborn."[2] After long conversations about the importance of this solemn oath, they prayed together and committed their firstborn to the Lord. His mother would later explain, "This act of consecration they solemnly performed upon their knees, asking for the rich

1. Pollock, *Taylor & Maria*, 189.
2. For example, Exod 13:1.

influence of the Holy Spirit" to set apart their first child for some special work of God.[3]

Hudson Taylor's father always carried a burden for China, and from Taylor's early years his father impressed upon him the needs of that great faraway land. Even when he was only four or five years old, Taylor was grieved to hear that many people in other countries lived in darkness and had no access to the gospel message. He often said, "When I am a man, I mean to be a missionary and go to China."[4]

It is fascinating that, in a day when becoming a missionary meant leaving home and never returning, Taylor's parents often prayed that their child would become a missionary. It was in fact their "chief desire"[5] that their son might be called to such service and be used of God for the spread of the gospel in China. Growing up in such a home, one that not only accepted the possibility of missionary service but also encouraged and embraced it, had an incalculable impact on Hudson Taylor's early years. Despite this enthusiasm, Taylor was frequently sick in his childhood. His parents considered his "continued delicacy" and slowly realized that his body simply wasn't strong enough for the rigors of missionary life.[6]

When he was fifteen, Taylor went through a period of skepticism and worldliness. Like many who grow up in Christian homes, he drifted away from the truths of Scripture that had so gripped him as a child. After obtaining a privileged position working at a bank, unbelieving coworkers influenced Taylor and led him to love the things of the world. He wrote of this period in a series of letters later in life.

> I well remember, how I used to wish for money and a fine horse and house when I was in the bank. Then my whole heart was set on this world's pleasures, and I longed to go hunting as some did who were about me. . . . I began

3. Taylor, *Early Years*, 34.
4. Taylor, *Early Years*, 37.
5. Taylor, *Early Years*, 52.
6. Taylor, *Early Years*.

to set too great a value on the things of this world, and to neglect private prayer. Religious duties became irksome to me, and I fell from grace. But God in His infinite mercy caused my eyesight to fail, and I had to leave the bank.[7]

After leaving the bank, though, Taylor was at home by himself on a holiday. Being bored and having nothing to do, he looked through his father's books to find something to read. Finding no books of interest, he picked up a gospel tract and thought there might be a story or parable at the end of the sermon. The pamphlet used the phrase, "The Finished Work of Christ," and Taylor began to think on that phrase and on the reality that Christ had paid his debt of sin and had completed his salvation, and he pondered how he should respond to such a concept. He later wrote, "There was nothing in the world for me to do save fall upon my knees and, accepting this Savior and His salvation, to praise Him for evermore."[8]

The amazing part of Taylor's conversion story is that, at that very moment when he started to read the tract, his mother was praying for him. At the time, she was eighty miles away and was eating dinner. Sensing a need to pray for her son, she confined herself to a solitary place and spent several hours in prayer for him. At the end of this prolonged period, she felt a sense of relief and assurance that her prayer had been answered. She immediately began praising God for her son's salvation.[9] Taylor would later write, "Thus while my dear mother was praising God on her knees in her chamber, I was praising him in the old warehouse to which I had gone to read at my leisure this little book."[10] Taylor would later discover that, a month prior to his conversion, his sister had also made a commitment to pray daily for her brother's salvation.[11] Reflecting on such miraculous circumstances, Taylor wrote:

7. Taylor, *Early Years*, 64.

8. Taylor, *Spiritual Secret*, 17.

9. Taylor, *Early Years*, 66–68.

10. Taylor, *Early Years*, 68.

11. Taylor, *Spiritual Secret*, 18.

> Brought up in such a circle and saved under such cir-
> cumstances, it was perhaps natural that from the very
> commencement of my Christian life I was led to feel that
> the promises of the Bible are very real, and that prayer
> is in sober fact transacting business with God, whether
> on one's behalf or on behalf of those for whom one seeks
> His blessing.[12]

After his dramatic conversion, Taylor experienced several years of spiritual growth. He wrote, "I besought Him to give me some work, as an outlet for love and gratitude; some self-denying service, no matter what it might be, however trying or however trivial."[13] To his sister he wrote, "I feel very happy in his love, but I am so unworthy of all His blessings. . . . The earnest desire of my heart is that He will sanctify me wholly and make me useful in His cause."[14] Then not long after, during a time of prayer, he heard a call as distinct as a voice speaking to him saying, "Then go for Me to China."[15] From that time forward, all his energy was focused on preparing for that specific task. He exercised more regularly, slept on a hard mattress, and ate less. He also began studying Chinese, a task so formidable a contemporary wrote it required "bodies of iron, lungs of brass, heads of oak, hands of steel, eyes of eagles, hearts of apostles, memories of angels, and lives of Methuselah."[16] Since he couldn't afford a grammar book, he found a copy of the Gospel of Luke in Chinese and compared the translation with the English equivalent. This painstaking study helped him to learn some 600 characters.[17]

Having read a book that emphasized the value of medical missions in China, Taylor began to study medicine.[18] Perhaps the most important lesson he learned during that period, though,

---

12. Taylor, *Spiritual Secret*, 5–6; Taylor, *Early Years*, 68.

13. Taylor, *Early Years*, 70.

14. Taylor, *Early Years*, 76.

15. Taylor, *Early Years*, 78.

16. Taylor, *Early Years*, 86.

17. Taylor, *Spiritual Secret*, 23–24.

18. Taylor, *Early Years*, 85

was the importance of prayer in every circumstance of life. Living on his own, studying medicine, and working as an apprentice to a doctor all provided Taylor with opportunities to trust Christ. He determined to never ask his employer for his salary but only to pray. Of that decision, he wrote, "How important, therefore, to learn before leaving England, to move man, through God, by prayer alone."[19]

On one occasion the doctor forgot to give Taylor his salary, and he was down to his last half-crown—one eighth of a pound. After leaving church on Sunday evening, he encountered a poor man whose wife was ill and near death, and the man requested Taylor to come and pray over her. While he was with the man, the Spirit began to urge him to give the man all his remaining money. He initially resisted, but upon seeing their desperation and hearing their pleas, the Spirit spoke to him saying, "Give to him that asketh of thee."[20] Though his money was gone and he knew not where his next few meals would come from, he was filled with joy. The next morning, while eating a leftover bowl of porridge, a letter came in the mail which contained a pair of gloves, and inside the gloves was a half-sovereign, four times the amount he had given away the night before. Reflecting on this event later in life Taylor explained the lesson.

> I cannot tell you how often my mind has recurred to this incident, or all the help it has been to me in circumstances of difficulty in afterlife. If we are faithful to God in little things, we shall gain experience and strength that will be helpful to us in the more serious trials of life.[21]

Taylor would later apply these lessons to his overall philosophy of missions, but at this point in his life he was still figuring out what his future missionary service might look like. When speaking with one minister and explaining that God had called him to be a missionary, the minister asked Taylor how he planned to support

19. Broomhall, *Shaping of Modern China*, 1:184–85.

20. Taylor, *Early Years*, 134.

21. Taylor, *Early Years*, 135. For a more detailed explanation of these events and other similar ones, see Taylor, *Early Years*, 132–38.

himself after being sent out. Taylor explained that he planned to depend on God to meet all his needs. Taylor explained the minister's skepticism.

> Kindly placing his hand on my shoulder, he replied, "Ah, my boy. As you grow older you will get wiser than that. Such an idea would do very well in the days when Christ Himself was on earth, but not now."[22]

Reflecting on this response later in life Taylor quipped, "I have grown older since then, but not wiser."[23]

While Taylor was learning these lessons on prayer and having conversations with a mission-sending organization, a rebellion had started in China. John Pollock explains the events:

> In the early summer of 1853 astonishing news reached Europe. An obscure Hakka from South China, called Hung, had been hailed as Emperor. He claimed to be a Christian, and named his fast-increasing empire the Heavenly Kingdom of Great Peace, 太平天国. After nearly two years' revolt the Chinese southern capital, Nanjing, had fallen in March 1853. The Heavenly King's armies were marching on Beijing. The alien Manchu dynasty tottered. The Dragon Throne might soon be held by a Christian.[24]

Up until this point, foreigners could only reside in a few port cities. Recognizing that the Taiping Rebellion could mean the opening up of China's interior and provide a new openness to Christianity with a Christian Emperor, the China Evangelization Society agreed to send Taylor to Shanghai. Although he hadn't finished his education and had little formal theological training, it was highly likely that in the next five years the organization's need of experienced, language-competent missionaries would be great.

---

22. Broomhall, *Shaping of Modern China*, 1:169

23. Broomhall, *Shaping of Modern China*.

24. Pollock, *Taylor & Maria*, 24. Hakas are an ethnic group that lives in Southern China.

China early years

On September 19, 1853, Taylor set sail from Liverpool. It would be five long months before Hudson Taylor once again set foot on land, when the boat made a brief stopover in Western Australia. Even then, it would be another three months before he arrived in Shanghai. On arrival he wrote, "My feelings on stepping ashore, I cannot attempt to describe. My heart felt as though it had not room and must burst its bonds, while tears of gratitude and thankfulness fell from my eyes."[25]

Despite the gratefulness and excitement that Taylor felt upon arrival, his first few years in China were exceedingly difficult. All the directors of the organization were in London, and as a result, they were unable to provide much insight or advice into how Taylor should go about his work. The organization was slow in providing the money that Taylor needed to live on. At a time when he should've been studying the language, Taylor then found himself finding housing and preparing for an additional family to join him—even though he barely had enough money to support himself. To make matters worse, Shanghai was a warzone. On one occasion when Taylor was on the roof of his home, bullets struck the neighboring houses, and before he could get down, a cannonball struck the adjacent roof, splaying roof tiles all over Taylor.

In addition to all these challenges, Taylor faced the difficulty that almost every missionary faces—loneliness. Though surrounded by great gospel needs at every corner, he was unable to converse well enough to do anything about it. Though he never wavered in his calling or commitment, that calling didn't make this challenge any less severe. Once, when mail arrived from home, he needed to pay to receive the letter. Taylor wrote, "Never did I pay two shillings more willingly in my life, than for that letter."[26] On another occasion he wrote, "I had the pleasure of bringing up letters and papers for everyone at the Mission except myself. When I found there really was nothing for me, the disappointment was so great I

25. Taylor, *Early Years*, 203.
26. Taylor, *Early Years*, 207.

felt quite sick and faint and could scarcely manage to walk home, for it was reported that we should have no other mail for six or eight weeks."[27]

Once Taylor began to speak the language more fluently, he began to make trips to the interior. It was illegal for Taylor to travel to many of these areas, but he was burdened by the gospel need and was willing to take the risk. On one trip, Taylor and his companion climbed a sacred mountain.

> Ascending from height to height, we passed shrine after shrine, and everywhere the same scene was repeated: idols, priests, worshippers. Heavy fumes of incense filled the air; and the clinking of cash, as the passers-by threw their coins into baskets placed before the idols mingled with strains of music, the buzz of conversation and tramp of passing feet. Upon reaching the summit we entered the halls connected with the pagoda, named from the temple *Tai-shan tan*, the hideous figures of the idols, seen through smoke and flames from burning paper, [Offerings of money and other objects made in paper, expressly for burning before the idols] making it seem like . . . a place where Satan's seat is.[28]

The lostness of the land was never far from Taylor's eyes.

While on these trips inland, Taylor began to realize the value of adopting Chinese dress and hairstyle. While wearing Western clothes afforded him certain privileges in society, dressing like the Chinese enabled Taylor to move about more freely and caused his listeners to pay closer attention to his gospel message. After cutting his hair in the local style, dying it black, and donning Chinese clothes, he found many new doors opened to him when traveling to the interior. At the same time, the missionary community in Shanghai was shocked and thought Taylor was losing his mind. One respected doctor described Taylor's actions as "objectionable" and expected that Chinese would respect him less.[29]

27. Taylor, *Early Years*, 222.

28. Taylor, *Early Years*, 285.

29. Pollock, *Taylor & Maria*, 56.

Few responded to Taylor's preaching of the gospel. He wrote to his sister, "I wish I could tell you of an outpouring of the Holy Spirit on this place. The Lord has not been pleased to grant this."[30] Although he saw few results to his labors for the gospel, Taylor never gave up and likewise never considered his efforts wasted. He continued to his sister, "So here, though we see not all we could wish at present, we know that our labor is 'not in vain in the Lord.'"[31]

Taylor then spent seven months traveling in the interior with William Burns, a Scottish preacher who helped lead the revival of 1839. Burns was the mentor that Taylor had always longed for, but the Lord made it clear to both that after this short period they should go their separate ways. After years of loneliness, accepting the Lord's will and parting ways with a trusted friend and mentor was painful, and Taylor would have never embraced this step apart from clear direction from the Lord. In God's providence after separating from Burns and relocating to Ningbo, Taylor entered one of his most fruitful and enjoyable seasons of ministry. During this time period, he met his first wife Maria and saw several converts who later became critical partners in ministry.

The lesson is an important one for all of us. There are many times in life when obedience to God's will is painful or difficult to accept. Even though God leads us to make these difficult decisions, he always blesses those who are faithful and are willing to accept and embrace God's plan over against the comforts of this world. The blessing doesn't always look like what we want it to, and it doesn't always come in the time or in the form or fashion that we desire. Nonetheless, he always blesses faithfulness with greater intimacy in our relationship with him, and often, with seasons of greater fruitfulness in ministry.

In January 1858, nearly four years after first arriving in China, Hudson Taylor married Maria Dyer. They would spend three years together in China before illness and fatigue forced them to return to England. Taylor spent a good part of those years investing in

30. Taylor, *Early Years*, 352.
31. Taylor, *Early Years*.

new converts. He taught them to read the Bible for themselves and often spent two hours a day teaching them and discussing biblical content with them.

One of those converts was a man named Ni, who was a Buddhist religious leader and president of a society of idolatry. He had spent much of his life in service of the gods, but his heart was not at rest. After hearing Taylor present the gospel, he said, "I have long sought the truth, but without finding it. I have travelled far and near, but I have never searched it out. In Confucianism, Buddhism, Taosim, I have found no rest. But I do find rest in what we have heard tonight. Henceforth, I am a believer in Jesus."[32] Later one of those converts would ask Taylor how long people in his country had known the gospel. Reporting that the gospel had been in England for hundreds of years, the man responded to Taylor saying, "My father sought the truth and died without finding it. Oh, why did you not come sooner?"[33] It was a question that Hudson Taylor would never forget.

China post-marriage

In 1861, Taylor and his young family returned to England. With all that he had experienced thus far in his life, it is amazing that at that time Taylor was only twenty-nine years of age and Maria only twenty-four. For someone like Taylor, who from such a young age felt the burden of millions in China who had yet to hear the gospel, leaving China was extremely difficult. It would be more than four years before he would be able to return, and he no doubt saw these years as wasted. The Lord, though, used the uncertainty and the challenges of those years to prepare him for future work.

While in London his zeal for getting the gospel to China never waned. His son described Taylor's perspective during these years, "The great need, as he had seen it, and a deep sense of responsibility burned as a steady fire in his soul, and neither poor health,

32. Taylor, *Spiritual Secret*, 93.
33. Taylor, *Spiritual Secret*, 94.

lack of encouragement, nor any other difficulty could lessen his sense of call to bring Christ to those perishing millions."[34] When he would speak to Christians in the West of the gospel needs in the East, he would often cause them to consider their own calling.

> Do you believe that each unit of these millions has an immortal soul, and that there is 'no other name under heaven given among men' save the precious name of Jesus 'whereby we must be saved'? Do you believe that He and He alone is 'the Way, the Truth, and the Life,' and that 'no man cometh unto the Father' but by Him? If so, think of the condition of these unsaved souls, and examine yourself in the sight of God to see whether you are doing your utmost to make Him known to them or not. It will not do to say that you have no special call to go to China. With these facts before you, you need rather to ascertain whether you have a special call to stay at home.[35]

Taylor himself was spending long hours translating the New Testament into the Ningbo dialect. In April of 1860, his journal records spending at least eight hours a day on editing and revising, and some days he spent as much eleven or twelve hours.[36] During this time, his burden grew beyond the lostness of Ningbo, Shanghai, and the other regions he had visited. Years later he explained how his vision increased.

> While on the field, the pressure of claims immediately around me was so great that I could not think much of the still greater need farther inland and could do nothing to meet it. But detained some years in England, daily viewing the whole country on the large map in my study, I was as near the vast regions of the interior as the smaller districts in which I had personally labored and prayer was the only resource by which the burdened heart could obtain any relief.[37]

34. Taylor, *Spiritual Secret*, 105.
35. Taylor, *China Inland Mission*, 7–8.
36. Taylor, *China Inland Mission*, 16–17.
37. Taylor, *China Inland Mission*, 23.

The burden for the unreached millions in inland China never lessened. Taylor explained the inward struggle he faced during those days.

> I knew God was speaking, I knew that in answer to prayer evangelists would be given and their support secured, because the Name of Jesus is worthy. But there unbelief came in. 'Suppose the workers are given and go to China: trials will come; their faith may fail; would they not reproach you for bringing them into such a plight? Have you ability to cope with so painful a situation?'. . . And I did not see that the power that would give the men and the means would be sufficient to keep them also, even in the far interior of China. Meanwhile, a million a month were dying in that land, dying without God. This was burned into my very soul. For two or three months the conflict was intense. I scarcely slept night or day more than an hour at a time, and feared I should lose my reason. Yet I did not give in.[38]

The breaking point came on June 25, 1865. Still in ill health, Taylor had gone to Brighton for a restful weekend. That Sunday morning the burden for China was so great that he could not bear to see some rejoicing in God while so many others had no access to the gospel. He wandered out onto the beach alone and made a commitment to do what God had been leading him to do for so many months—found a new organization whose goal would be the evangelization of inland China. Standing on the beach he began to pray, "Thou, Lord, thou shalt have all the burden! At thy bidding, as thy servant I go forward, leaving the results with thee."[39] At that moment he wrote in his Bible: "Prayed for twenty-four willing skillful laborers at Brighton,"[40] that is, two workers for each unoccupied province in China.

To accomplish this purpose or securing workers for every province in China, Taylor wrote *China's Spiritual Need and Claims*,

38. Taylor, *China Inland Mission*, 30–31.
39. Taylor, *China Inland Mission*, 32.
40. Taylor, *China Inland Mission*.

and sought to confront Christians with the gospel needs of China. He hoped the book would provoke them to do something to help make the gospel available to the people of China. In the book, he placed many statistics before the reader and wrote that he hoped these facts would produce a certain kind of fruit. This "legitimate fruit will undoubtedly be—not vain words of empty sympathy, but—effectual fervent prayer, and strenuous self-denying effort for the salvation of the Chinese."[41]

Writing about China, he reasoned, "Let us reflect on its great antiquity, its vast extent, its teeming population; on its spiritual destitution, and overwhelming need."[42] He continued, "It is surely high time that this ancient and most interesting empire had the gospel fully proclaimed in its purity and soul-saving power. . . . No other nation has been left for so many centuries to suffer in darkness, and to prove how utterly unable man is to raise himself without divine revelation, and the regenerating power of the Holy Spirit."[43]

Building on the lessons Taylor had learned during his first seven years in China, the mission strategy of the China Inland Mission (CIM) would be based on several principles. First, they would adopt Chinese dress. Though rejected by other missionaries as foolhardy, Taylor had found this approach to be the best way to gain access to the inland areas. Second, the directors of their work would live in China. Taylor had learned the hard way that when mission directors lived in England, they were ill-equipped to provide guidance on issues related to the Chinese context. Third, they would operate on a faith principle. Taylor had learned during his days as an apprentice that by prayer, God was more than able to supply all their needs. Finally, there would be no requirements for education, denominational background, or marital status. They would even welcome single females, which was a highly controversial decision.

---

41. Taylor, *China's Spiritual Need and Claims*, 1.
42. Taylor, *China's Spiritual Need and Claims*, 3.
43. Taylor, *China's Spiritual Need and Claims*.

Given the isolation, dangers, and setbacks that they encountered in sending missionaries to the interior, unreached parts of China, Taylor also came to the conclusion that for married couples, both husband and wife must share the same calling. He later wrote home from the field:

> We aim at the interior, where the whole of your society will be Chinese. If you wish for luxury and freedom from care . . . do not join us. Unless you intend your wife to be a true missionary, not merely a wife, home-maker, and friend, do not join us. She must be able to read and be a master of at least one Gospel in colloquial Chinese before you marry. A person of ordinary ability may accomplish this in six months, but if she needs longer there is the more reason to wait until she has reached this point before you marry. She must be prepared to be happy among the Chinese when the duties of your calling require, as they often will, your temporary absence from home. You, too, must master the initial difficulties of the language and open up a station, if none be allotted to you, before you marry. With diligence and God's blessing you may hope to do this in a year or so. If these conditions seem too hard, these sacrifices too great to make for perishing China, do not join our Mission. These are small things to some of the crosses you may be permitted to bear for your dear Master![44]

He went on to write, "China is not to be won for Christ by self-seeking, ease-loving men and women. Those not prepared for labor, self-denial, and many discouragements will be poor helpers in the work. In short, the men and women we need are those who will put Jesus, China, souls first and foremost in everything and at all times: life itself must be secondary—nay, even those more precious than life. Of such men, of such women, do not fear to send us too many. Their price is far above rubies."[45]

Taylor would lead the CIM for the next thirty-seven years. He endured unimaginable suffering during those years. He was

---

44. Taylor, *China Inland Mission*, 156.

45. Taylor, *China Inland Mission*.

criticized in England for sending single females. Some missionaries rebelled against his leadership and mission principles. Once
while he was traveling, a riot erupted and the rioters threatened
the lives of his wife, children, and multiple coworkers. The difficulties of life in China had a massive impact on his health. The
hardships took the life of his wife and multiple children. Later in
1900, during an uprising against foreign influence called the Boxer
Rebellion, fifty-eight CIM missionaries and twenty-one children
were killed. Thousands of Chinese Christians were also killed during that period.

And yet, in spite of all these challenges, CIM became the largest mission organization in the world. Much more could be said
of Taylor's simple faith, his relentless work ethic, his willingness
to wake up at 3:00 AM for devotions, and his emphasis on abiding
in Christ. By the turn of the century CIM supported more than
600 missionaries in every province in China. At that point in his
life, an admirer asked Taylor if he was proud of his work since he
certainly had every reason to be proud of what he'd accomplished
for God. "On the contrary," replied Taylor, "I often think God must
have been looking for someone small enough and weak enough
for Him to use, and that he found me."[46]

LOVE SACRIFICED

Hudson Taylor was not perfect. We have already seen that he
struggled with loneliness, and in addition, the pressures and
stresses of his work left him frustrated, depressed, or angry. One
biographer wrote of a time early in the days of the CIM when
Taylor was near suicidal.[47] What is so inspirational about his story
is not simply that he overcame these challenges through faith or
that he accomplished much for the Lord. What is inspirational is
that throughout his life he was willing to sacrifice the things of
this world that most people hold dear to embrace better the will

46. Taylor, *Spiritual Secret*, 201–2; Pollock, *Taylor & Maria*, 141.
47. Pollock, *Taylor & Maria*, 220.

of God. More than that, he was willing to place himself and those he loved at risk for the sake of getting the gospel to those who had never heard.

Marianne Vaughn and Elizabeth Sissons

We have already seen that Hudson Taylor was called to missions at a young age and spent most of his youth preparing for the work he would later do in China. When he was seventeen, his younger sister Amelia brought home a friend named Marianne Vaughn with her for Christmas. She was a music teacher at the school where Amelia was studying and by the end of the holiday, Taylor was in love.

Even though he had no idea how she felt, he was immediately perplexed. At his young age with all his attention focused on preparing for China, he had no way to support a wife even if she was interested in him. Perhaps the more complex question was whether or not she would share or embrace his calling. If she *was* interested in him, would she also be interested in China? A year after he first met her he wrote to his sister, "I know I love her. To go [to China] without her would make the world a blank."[48]

In time, Taylor would realize that Miss V, as he affectionately referred to her in his journals and letters, shared his feelings. She did not, however, share his call. In their conversations she often asked him, "Must you go to China?"[49] As one biographer put it, "The music-teacher had no intention of going to China; this absurd ambition must wither under the strong sun of her charms."[50] Her mother was not healthy, and she needed to be nearby to help care for her. With the added stress of a sick wife, the thought of her departure to a foreign country was unbearable for her father. Moreover, she did not see herself equipped for the difficulties of

---

48. Pollock, *Taylor & Maria*, 20.
49. Broomhall, *Shaping of Modern China*, 1:176.
50. Pollock, *Taylor & Maria*, 20.

missionary life. And yet, for his part, Taylor thought he could eventually persuade her to change her mind.[51]

Throughout these several years, Hudson Taylor was in anguish and struggled to understand which direction God was leading him. On the one hand, he knew that he and Marianne Vaughn were in love, but on the other hand, he knew that she did not share his calling. He wrote to his mother, "I try to subdue my will, but I seem to have an impression that I shall lose my dear Miss V . . . I have to say, 'Nevertheless, not my will but *thine* be done.'"[52] In that same letter he conveyed how difficult it was "to set our affections wholly on things above."[53] In his journal he penned the inner struggle of those days.

> [I felt] . . . as wretched as heart could wish. I seemed as if I had no power in prayer nor relish for it, and instead kept it all myself until I could get on no longer, on Sunday I felt no desire to go to Meeting and was tempted very much. Satan seemed to come in like a flood, till I was forced to cry mentally "Save Lord, or I perish" . . . but thank God "the way of duty is the way of safety," and I went. . . . [Later that day] the thoughts of His love melted my icy, frost-bound soul, and I did sincerely pray for pardon. . . . Then, though He did not deprive me of feeling my trials, He enabled me to sing, "Yet, notwithstanding, I will rejoice in the Lord, I will joy in the God of my salvation."[54]

It is fascinating to note that during these days of trial, Taylor's journal records the fact that he was reading Henry Martyn's journal. One can only imagine how Martyn's decision to lay aside earthly love to leave for India affected Taylor's perspective during these days.

---

51. Broomhall, *Shaping of Modern China*, 1:179–80; 201.
52. Broomhall, *Shaping of Modern China*, 1:175.
53. Taylor, *Early Years*, 114.
54. Broomhall, *Shaping of Modern China*, 1:179–80.

On another occasion when Marianne had told him she would not commit to China, Taylor was dejected and depressed. That morning he was plagued by a simple series of questions.

> 'Is it all worthwhile? Why should you go to China? Why toil and suffer all your life for an ideal of duty? Give it up now, while you can yet win her. Earn a proper living like everybody else, and serve the Lord at home. For you can win her yet.' Love pleaded hard. It was a moment of wavering and peril. The enemy came in like a flood. But enough! The Spirit of the Lord lifted up a standard against him.[55]

While their affections were growing for one another, Taylor was studying medicine and was one day assigned to dissect a body that had died from fever. Forgetting that he had pricked his finger the night before, Taylor suddenly became weary, and only then realized that he had become infected with the very fever that had killed this patient. The surgeon in charge told him, "You are a dead man." Taylor responded, "Unless I am greatly mistaken, I have work to do in China and shall not die."[56] Taylor would recover, and apparently this event deepened the love between him and Marianne because the next entry in his journal reveals that they were engaged with her father's approval. Moreover, Marianne had agreed to go to China and was preparing with him to be sent out.[57]

Two months later, though, Taylor realized that Marianne was avoiding him and wrote to his sister, "I know she does not love me as she did. She says all her friends are against our union, and they all tell her she is doing very wrong to think of going abroad without her parents' assent."[58] When they finally met together, they agreed to write to Mr. Vaughn and ask his opinion. In his reply, he told Taylor that had he "been going to remain in England, nothing would have given him more pleasure than to have seen us happily united but that, though he did not forbid our connection, he felt he

55. Taylor, *Early Years*, 123.
56. Taylor, *Early Years*, 165.
57. Broomhall, *Shaping of Modern China*, 1:198–99.
58. Broomhall, *Shaping of Modern China*, 1:200.

never could willingly give her up, or even think of her leaving this country, etc. etc."[59] Mr. Vaughn had changed his mind, thus Taylor and Marianne made the mutual decision of breaking off their engagement. He wrote to his sister, "I cannot help loving her and believe she loves me. However, it is in the Lord's hands and if he sees fit he can remove the obstacles, and if not—his will be done."[60]

This first great sacrifice that Taylor made in obedience to the call of God had been excruciatingly painful. And yet, later in life, when considering a life filled with sacrifice, he would strangely say, "I never made a sacrifice."[61] His son explained how Taylor could make such a statement when he wrote, "Not outwardly only but inwardly also he had accepted the will of God, giving up what seemed his best and highest, the love that had become part of his very life, that he might be unhindered in following Christ."[62] Unhindered in following Christ—this phrase gets to the heart of why Taylor could say he never made a sacrifice. He saw these events as a sort of transaction. Certainly, giving up one thing he loved and wanted was difficult, but if giving up that thing enabled him to serve Christ more faithfully, he was more than willing to give it up.

In the section above we saw how Taylor struggled so much in the first few years in China with loneliness. Though he knew he had lost Marianne for good, he longed for the companionship of a wife. He wrote to his sister of these thoughts and said, "Whatever I set my heart on, I lose. I thought Miss V would prove an exception but it was not so."[63] Though still heartbroken at the thought of losing her, a year on the field had helped him see the wisdom in God's plan, "I see she is not fit for a missionary's wife."[64]

At this point in his life, he began to consider a possible match with another of his sister's friends, Elizabeth Sissons. She had comforted Taylor after his engagement had been broken off, and

59. Broomhall, *Shaping of Modern China*, 1:201

60. Broomhall, *Shaping of Modern China*.

61. Taylor, *Early Years*, 126.

62. Taylor, *Spiritual Secret*, 30.

63. Pollock, *Taylor & Maria*, 37.

64. Pollock, *Taylor & Maria*.

during his first year in China, he wrote to her requesting a lock of her hair.[65] He would later send her a formal offer of marriage, which she would tentatively accept, given that her father thought it best for her to wait to join him in China.[66] Taylor, at that time, was just beginning to realize his passion for the interior of China. A new inner struggle raged at the recognition that Miss Sissons was not the kind of woman who could handle life in the interior and marriage to her would mean abandoning the call of God to the interior for a life in a coastal city like Shanghai. Once again Taylor was at a crossroads where his worldly desires were in conflict with the call of God.

In this case, he didn't need to decide. Kicked out of an interior area and returning by boat to Shanghai, Taylor heard that mail had arrived from England. Tearing open a letter from Elizabeth he read that she feared she no longer loved him.[67] Perhaps more accurately we can say that she did not love him *enough* to leave the comforts of home and embrace the difficulties of life in China. Taylor, understandably, was dejected and once again began to wonder if he would ever find a suitable wife. From our perspective, though, we can once again see the wisdom of God in these events. For as one biographer notes, this love "would have snuffed out the flame of his pioneering zeal."[68]

Maria Dyer

During the period of his life when he was corresponding with Elizabeth Sissons, Taylor made his first visit to Ningbo. He was impressed with the missionary community there but failed to even notice a beautiful young girl that was ministering in the girls' school run by those missionaries. Maria Dyer was the child of missionary parents. Her father, a contemporary of Robert Morrison,

65. Pollock, *Taylor & Maria*.

66. Pollock, *Taylor & Maria*, 51, 56.

67. Pollock, *Taylor & Maria*, 65.

68. Pollock, *Taylor & Maria*, 73.

was burdened for China, but was unable to gain access to that great land. He developed the typesetting process for printing Chinese characters, thus enabling the printing of the first Chinese Bible. After traveling from Malacca, Malaysia to Hong Kong for a meeting, he developed a fever and passed away. Her mother remarried, but when Maria was nine years old her mother died also. Maria and her brother returned to England. When she was sixteen she made the decision to move to China with her older sister and work at the girls' school in Ningbo.

Before Taylor relocated to Ningbo, he was traveling with William Burns, and it was a painful act of obedience for him to leave Burns and move to Ningbo. That painful act, though, led to great blessing when he met Maria. For her, teaching at the girls' school was much more than just an academic exercise. She understood that the heartbeat of mission work was the sharing of the gospel and the planting of churches. Since she had this perspective, Taylor, when he did finally notice her, was immediately attracted to her. Though Taylor had been attracted and had even proposed to two others before Maria, they never shared his passion and commitment to the work. It was this unity of purpose that drew him and Maria together, though their love for one another was not without opposition.

While in Ningbo, Maria was under the care of Miss Aldersey, the matriarch of the Ningbo missionary community, having been the first to open a girls' school in China in 1843. Being a gentleman, when Taylor began to have feelings for Maria, he approached Miss Aldersey to gain her approval for further communication. Maria was secretly excited to learn of Taylor's interest, but Miss Aldersey's reaction was the opposite. She responded in angst, "Mr. Taylor! That young, poor, unconnected nobody. How dare he presume to think of such a thing? Of course the proposal must be refused at once, and that finally."[69] Putting her thoughts in writing, she explained to Maria, "Once more I come to you dear Maria as your faithful monitor, warning you against the mad step to which

69. Taylor, *Spiritual Secret*, 85–86.

a strange infatuation characterized by and endorsed by religious romance appears to be hastening you."[70]

Miss Aldersey, along with many of the other missionaries, thought Taylor was mad for dying his red hair black and adopting Chinese dress. Moreover, he had no formal education or degree like most other missionaries. In Miss Aldersey's mind, these issues made Taylor a terrible match for Maria. She forced Maria to write a reply stating her lack of interest in Taylor. He saw through the act, and recognized that though the handwriting was Maria's, the voice was Miss Aldersey's.

After writing the response, Maria's interest in Taylor only increased. As a result, Taylor wrote home that others in the missionary community "charged [Maria] with being a maniac, being fanatical, being indecent, weak-minded, too easily swayed; too obstinate and everything else bad."[71] Maria, though, recognized that degrees or worldly recognition was not what made a quality match. She responded, "I would wait if he went home in order to increase his usefulness. But is he to leave his work in order to gain a *name* for the sake of marrying me? If he loves me more than Jesus he is not worthy of me—if he were to leave the *Lord's* work for the *world's* honor, I would have nothing further to do with him."[72]

Not being Maria's official guardian, the decision ultimately did not belong to Miss Aldersey. In an attempt to end this discussion once and for all, then, she wrote to Maria's actual guardian in England explaining all the flaws in Taylor's character. Taylor for his part also wrote to Maria's guardian, pleading his case. In the meantime, all Taylor and Maria could do was wait. From our perspective, it may seem strange to wait so long for their parents' approval. For Taylor, this approval wasn't a matter of tradition or cultural etiquette, but it was a recognition that God had placed their parents in a position of authority over them. Later in life he explained that obedience to them was obedience to God: "I have never known disobedience to the definite command of a parent,

70. Pollock, *Taylor & Maria*, 102.

71. Pollock, *Taylor & Maria*.

72. Pollock, *Taylor & Maria*.

even if that parent were mistaken, that was not followed by retribution. Conquer through the Lord. He can open any door."[73] While Hudson and Maria awaited the response, both committed themselves to pray and trust the Lord with their futures.

At this point, Taylor had already left the China Evangelization Society and had adopted a faith approach to missions. Miss Aldersey attacked Taylor's character in the missionary community by ridiculing this approach saying that he was "called by no one, connected with no one, and recognized by no one as a minister of the gospel."[74] She went on to say that he was "fanatical, undependable, diseased in body and mind, and totally worthless."[75] Taylor found refuge in God alone. Maria too, as she found comfort in the promises of Scripture, "Trust in Him at all times; ye people, pour out your hearts before Him: God is a refuge for us."[76]

Upon receiving the letters, Maria's guardian conducted his own investigation, and found no reason to forbid the match. He wrote to Maria saying, "We certainly have not heard anything to induce us to oppose your wishes." He went on, "It is impossible for us to judge the suitability of Mr. Taylor to be your husband . . . and therefore can only leave you in the Lord's hands . . . guiding you to do what is right and preserving you from what is wrong."[77] He wrote a similar letter to Taylor explaining that many in England spoke positively of Taylor, "The testimonies of these gentlemen are as favorable as we could wish and such as to lead us to approve of the proposed union." They themselves had some difficulty understanding Taylor's faith approach and why he felt the necessity to leave the China Evangelization Society, but he explained that the CES committee members spoke highly of Taylor in spite of their break. His only requirement was that Taylor and Maria wait until her twenty-first birthday, then only a few months away.

73. Taylor, *Spiritual Secret*, 88–89.
74. Taylor, *Early Years*, 437.
75. Taylor, *Early Years*.
76. Taylor, *Early Years*, 438.
77. Broomhall, *Shaping of Modern China*, 1:435–36.

Taylor saw this response as an answer to prayer. He wrote, "God has been good to us. He has indeed answered our prayer and taken our part against the mighty. Oh, may we walk more closely with Him and serve Him more faithfully."[78] In the days leading up to their wedding, though, they encountered significant financial difficulties. They were helping the poor so much that they had little money left to pay for the wedding. One night Taylor took Maria's hand and gave her the opportunity to break off the engagement: "I cannot hold you to your promise if you would rather draw back. You see how difficult our life may be at times." Displaying their unity of mind and purpose, Maria replied, "Have you forgotten? I was left an orphan in a far-off land. God has been my Father all these years. Do you think I shall be afraid to trust Him now?"[79]

Though their first years of marriage continued to be filled with difficulty, they were years that were filled with happiness, primarily because they were together in the Lord and because they loved the work they were doing. Taylor wrote home to his mother during that first year of marriage and said, "I cannot tell you how much I love my precious wife. I am fully satisfied in her . . . perfection is nearer come to in her than I ever expected."[80] So satisfied was he in her that he feared he might forget to trust the Lord with the same level of intensity that he had during times of trial. He explained to his mother, "There is great danger of not, in happiness, finding our delight in the Lord, as in sorrow and trial."[81]

Two years later they would return to England so that Taylor's health could recover. It was during that period that Taylor's burden for inland China grew to the extent that he would write, "Every day tens of thousands in that land were passing into Christless graves! Perishing China so filled my heart and mind that there was no rest by day and little sleep by night."[82] Taylor only found relief when he

---

78. Taylor, *Spiritual Secret*, 89–90.

79. Pollock, *Taylor & Maria*, 112.

80. Broomhall, *Shaping of Modern China*, 1:443.

81. Broomhall, *Shaping of Modern China*.

82. Taylor, *Spiritual Secret*, 111.

submitted himself to the Lord's will and started the China Inland Mission. Their son explained Maria's help during those years:

> Frail in health and only twenty-eight years of age, Mrs. Taylor's hands were full with the care of four young children, yet from the moment she learned of her husband's call to the great, the seemingly impossible, task of the evangelization of inland China she became in a new way his comfort and inspiration. Her hand wrote for him, her faith strengthened his own, her prayers undergirded the whole work and her practical experience and loving heart made her the Mother of the Mission.[83]

The early years of leading the China Inland Mission together were filled with difficulty. One of the more heart-wrenching events was the death of the Taylor's oldest child Grace during their first year back. In consistent temperatures of 102 °F, Maria and the children became ill and were near death. Traveling by boat to a cooler location, Maria was so sick she needed to be carried up the steps. Upon arriving, though, Grace developed a fever and never recovered. Because of the superstitious beliefs in China related to departed spirits, Taylor and a coworker had to carry her body out of that place in the middle of the night. When they finally returned home and buried her, Maria penned the words:

> Renew my will from day today;
> Blend it with Thine, and take away
> All that now makes it hard to say
> Thy will be done.[84]

Three years later, in 1870, the Taylors sent their four oldest children back to England. The pain of this parting was compounded later that year when Maria gave birth to a baby boy. Shortly after giving birth, she developed cholera and was unable to nurse. Baby Noel passed away just one week later. Maria herself chose the hymn, "O holy Savior, Friend Unseen," to sing at his funeral.

---

83. Taylor, *Spiritual Secret*, 115.
84. Broomhall, *Shaping of Modern China*, 1:815.

> Though faith and hope are often tried,
> We ask not, need not, aught beside;
> So safe, so calm, so satisfied,
> The souls that cling to thee
>
> They fear not Satan nor the grave,
> They know. Thee near, and strong to save;
> Nor fear to cross e'en Jordan's wave,
> While still they cling to thee.[85]

Maria never recovered from the illness. As she lay dying, she looked up to Taylor and said simply, "I am so sorry." Taylor responded by asking if she was sorry that she'd soon be with Jesus. She told him, "Oh, no! It is not that. You know, darling, that for ten years past there has not been a cloud between me and my Savior. I cannot be sorry to go to Him; but it does grieve me to leave you alone at such a time. Yet . . . He will be with you and meet all your need."[86]

Twice earlier in his life Taylor's commitment to God's work led him to sacrifice love when others didn't share his passion. And now, after twelve years of sharing that work with one who shared his passion in the fullest sense, he was called to make another sacrifice. The hardships of missionary life and the difficulties of life on the field took away the one he loved more than any other. Though the sacrifice was great, Taylor looked to the Lord and trusted in his goodness. That final night, as Maria's breathing grew weaker, he "committed her to the Lord; thanking him for having given her, and for the twelve and a half years of happiness they had had together; thanking him, too, for taking her to his own blessed Presence, and solemnly dedicating himself anew to his service."[87] Then, the next day, as they placed her body in the coffin, Taylor spoke the words, "The Lord gave, and the Lord has taken away. Blessed be the name of the Lord."[88]

---

85. Taylor, *China Inland Mission*, 195.
86. Taylor, *China Inland Mission*, 197.
87. Pollock, *Taylor & Maria*, 232.
88. Pollock, *Taylor & Maria*. Cf. Job 1:21.

Hudson and Maria's love was special because they shared a unity of purpose. They loved the Lord and longed for others in inland China to know him and have a relationship with him. Maria's final act on earth was to point Taylor to God, reminding him of their shared work. With words that show the mingling of sorrow and hope, Taylor wrote in the days following her death:

> He and he only knew what my dear wife was to me. He knew how the light of my eyes and the joy of my heart were in her. On the last day of her life (we had no idea that it would prove the last) our hearts were mutually delighted by the never old story of each other's love, as they were every day, nearly; and almost her last act was, with one arm round my neck, to place her hand upon my head, and, as I believe, for her lips had lost their cunning, to implore a blessing on me. But he saw that it was good to take her; good indeed for her, and in his love he took her painlessly; and not less good for me who must henceforth toil and suffer alone-yet not alone, for God is nearer to me than ever. And now I have to tell him all my sorrows and difficulties, as I used to tell dear Maria; and as she cannot join me in intercession, to rest in the knowledge of Jesus' intercession; to walk a little less by feeling, a little less by sight, a little more by faith.[89]

Jennie Faulding

In the year following Maria's death, Taylor continued to deal with frequent bouts of dysentery and other severe illness. He also once again dealt with depression and loneliness. A verse that comforted him during those days was John 4:14: "Whoever drinks of the water I will give him will never be thirsty again." He wrote that many days, he felt "thirsty" some twenty times a day, and each time would cry out to the Lord for comfort. He wrote, "And whether I

89. Taylor, *China Inland Mission*, 199.

called by day or night, how quickly he always came and satisfied my sorrowing heart!"[90]

Eventually the health issues became too severe and Taylor needed to return to England both to rest and to visit his children. Returning on the same boat to England was another CIM missionary, Jennie Faulding. Jennie had been on the initial CIM team that was sent to China in 1866. Her parents had reservations about her living in China as a single female, but eventually gave in. Before leaving, she penned a note to Maria Taylor saying, "I am feeling very much what a trial it will be to leave England, but I long to be in China. . . . Oh that we may all be filled with the Spirit!"[91] In the five years she spent in China, she had become one of the Taylors' most faithful coworkers.

After Maria's death, Taylor began to depend more on Jennie for completion of his administrative tasks, especially those that related to the many single female missionaries in the CIM. When they both left for England and found themselves traveling on the same ship, it was only natural that they should confess their feelings for one another. Taylor wrote to her parents:

> You know the affections with which I and my late dear wife watched over her, prayed for her, and desired to do all we could (for her). . . . Nor will you deem it unnatural that when I found myself week to week more and more unable to carry on efficiently the work which the Lord has committed to me, my thoughts and prayers respecting the only one possessed at once of the heart for the Lord's service and of that peculiar preparation for sharing my peculiar duties, should unconsciously been . . . intensified.[92]

Taylor summarized his thoughts by saying, "My feelings could no longer be hid."[93] Jennie's parents initially opposed the union, fearing that neither one was physically fit for marriage. Perhaps

90. Taylor, *China Inland Mission*, 200.
91. Broomhall, *Shaping of Modern China*, 1:698.
92. Broomhall, *Shaping of Modern China*, 2:172.
93. Broomhall, *Shaping of Modern China*.

her parents recognized that marriage to Taylor would mean Jennie would not remain in England as they hoped. Taylor, for his part, had flashbacks to Miss Aldersey's intervention and opposition of his first marriage. Eventually, though, Jennie's parents agreed, and they were married.

Like Maria before her, Jennie became Taylor's partner in the work. They were well-suited for one another because they had a unity of purpose in getting the gospel to the lost of China. In fact, not long after first arriving in China Jennie wrote home, "I cannot tell you what a thrill of joy one constantly feels at the sight of so many heathen listening to the gospel."[94] And for Taylor, there was a great comfort in the fact that Jennie had known, and loved, his Maria. There was no shame, then, in holding back a part of his heart for her. He wrote to a friend shortly after their marriage:

> The last wish (Maria) expressed to me was that if she were
> removed, I would marry again. . . . Seeing the love I have
> for her is not likely to undergo any change or diminu-
> tion, I do not want one or two years, or five, to forget her
> in. You do not know how I love her, nor how seldom for
> one hour she is absent from my waking thoughts . . . And
> my dear (Jennie) would not wish it otherwise. She has
> her own place in my heart, which Jesus has given her, a
> place all the larger because her love is not jealous.[95]

Hudson and Jennie would be married and would lead the CIM together for more than thirty years. And then, a year before his own death, Jennie preceded him. On her deathbed, she was asked if she thought much about heaven, and she responded, "The Bible says more about [Christ] than it does about heaven. No, I do not often think of heaven. He is here with me, and he is enough."[96] Much like the peace that Maria experienced in her final days, Jennie was calm and asked Hudson Taylor to pray that the end would come quickly. Though grieving and heartbroken at the funeral, Taylor emphasized that Jennie had "entered into the joy

94. Taylor, *China Inland Mission*, 102.
95. Broomhall, *Shaping of Modern China*, 2:175.
96. Broomhall, *Shaping of Modern China*, 2:743.

of her Lord," and often referred to her burial site as "sacred until resurrection morning."[97]

Hudson Taylor's life was defined by one all consuming passion—to get the gospel to the unreached peoples of China. While still studying medicine and preparing to go to China the first time, he wrote to his sister, "I almost wish I had a hundred bodies; they should all be devoted to my Savior in the missionary cause."[98] Every decision he made was directed toward this one single goal. Twice in his youth he sacrificed earthly love because it would have kept him from going to China or would have limited his ability to do that work faithfully. Later in life, the commitment to his work once again required him to sacrifice his dearest on the altar of Christ. Maria's death was the most painful event of his adult life, and yet, the Lord used that event to increase Taylor's dependence on Christ and renew his commitment to the work.

In contrast to the other two subjects of this book, Taylor did get married—twice. Taylor's story is different from Martyn and Moon in that while he too sacrificed earthy love for the cause of Christ, he also found it while in the Lord's service. Nonetheless, while he loved Maria and Jennie greatly, their mutual commitment to Christ and to the advance of his kingdom served as the foundation for their love.

QUESTIONS FOR CONSIDERATION

1. Did you find it fascinating that while he was still young Taylor's parents prayed that he would become a missionary? How does this act of sacrificial love—that they were willing to send their son to the mission field—relate to the sacrificial love Taylor eventually displayed in his life?

2. After feeling called to China, in what ways did Taylor prepare for this work? How is his commitment to preparation

97. Broomhall, *Shaping of Modern China*, 1:743–44.
98. Broomhall, *Shaping of Modern China*, 1:182.

different from the ways many people today approach short-term missions?

3. What were some of the challenges Taylor faced in his first few years in China? Which of these challenges are similar to those that missionaries face today?

4. After marrying Maria, why did Taylor return to England in 1861? How do you think Taylor felt when he had to leave China? How did God use his time in England? What does Taylor's experience during these years teach us about how God often uses difficult circumstances in our lives?

5. One biographer wrote that with Marianne Vaughn, Taylor had given up "the love that had become part of his very life." How does Taylor's sacrifice compare to the way many people today treat true love? Which perspective is more biblical?

6. From our perspective, how can we see the hand of God guiding Taylor through the heartbreak of Marianne Vaughn and Elizabeth Sissons? How much did Taylor understand at the time? What lesson can we learn about trusting God in such circumstances?

7. Taylor's story is unique among these three because he eventually did get married. What can his courtship and marriage to Maria Dyer teach us about God's plan for marriage?

8. How is was Taylor's loss of Maria different from the other sacrifices he was called to make? Considering all the hardships and difficulties he faced during his time in China, why do you think he would say he never made a sacrifice?

5

Love for Christ Above All Others

I'LL NEVER FORGET THE day the Lord called me to missions. I was twenty years old and was five months away from graduating from college. A group of us had traveled to Taiwan and were sharing the gospel with college students there. Those students told us, "Since you shared your religion with us, we want to share our religion with you," and then took us to a Chinese temple. The sights and smells of that place are still seared into my memory, and I was broken by the time I left.

In the temple, people were banging cymbals and making loud noises in the hopes of warding off evil spirits. People were burning incense as they sought to gain blessing for themselves or for deceased ancestors. I saw a woman holding two crescent shaped blocks of wood. One side of the crescent was flat and the other side was curved. The woman held the blocks in her hand and threw them on the floor. Then she picked them up, held them a while, and threw them again.

The student next to me explained that this process was used for decision-making. The woman tossing the blocks was considering important decisions in her life, like "Should my son attend university?" or "Should I move to another city to better care for my mother?" She would ask the gods for direction and guidance, and then, if the blocks landed with one turned up and one turned down, she would have permission from the gods to move forward.

As I stood in the temple, I was struck with the hopelessness of the situation. Even today it is difficult to put in to words all that I experienced in that moment. Not only did the people in the temple not have certainty about the minute decisions of their lives, but they also didn't have certainty about eternity either. The practices in the temple made it clear that adherents of this religion had no assurance that any of these rituals would make a difference. These worshippers were hopeless wanderers, obeying traditions and rituals they did not understand and which benefited them none. These rituals were nothing but lame attempts to deal with the reality before these people—that their relationship with the Creator God was broken.

By the time I left the temple, I was having difficult processing all that I had seen. Never before had I witnessed such hopelessness and spiritual darkness. Never before had I seen people bowing down to idols. I walked away considering the words of the prophet Isaiah who wrote, "Their land is filled with idols. They bow down to the work of their hands, to what their own fingers have made" (Isa 2:8). How can there be hope and peace and joy for a people who focus their affections and effort on a block of wood? I knew that this experience would have an impact on my future, but at the time I wasn't sure what it all meant. Seeing the lostness around me, I could only consider this question: "How can I live in the same way I lived before?"

CALLING

So far we've considered here the lives of two men and one woman who came to a point in their lives when they considered that same question. At a young age, Hudson Taylor heard the voice of God telling him to go to China. He then spent all of his teenage years preparing to go. Henry Martyn heard a sermon about William Carey and knew from that moment that God was calling him to India. He spent three years in preparation and faced much opposition from family and friends. Though many sought to persuade him to stay in England, Martyn was certain of his calling and knew that he could not continue to live in the same way as he had before. Lottie Moon, too, when she heard John Broadus preach on missions, she knew that God was calling her to it. Since at that time no outlet existed for single females to go to the field, she had to wait some years before being sent. Faced with the needs before her, though, her life was not the same. She spent those years praying for and supporting those who were already on the field.

This book, though, is not just an academic study of what three people did in the past. The hope of this book is that God would use this study of their lives to inspire us to greater faithfulness and Great Commission obedience. You may or may not be called to pack up all your things and move to another country like the people in this book did. Even if you aren't though, you *are* called to be a Great Commission Christian. No matter what, you are called to pray for the peoples in the world who have little to no access to the gospel. No matter what, you are called to give to support those people sent out by your churches. No matter what, you are called to share the gospel with those in your community—and not just those in your community who share your cultural background, but also those of different ethnicities.

Doing so will require all of us to make sacrifices. Even if you are not called to go out for the sake of the gospel, you will need to make some difficult choices in life. We might ask ourselves if we really need new shoes, a new purse, a new phone, a new car, or a new whatever. What if I instead I use the old item for a bit longer and give the money I save to the missionary sent out from our church? What if instead of paying for someone else to make my coffee each morning, I start making it myself? Doing so requires more effort and time on my part, but by doing so I'm able to give the extra money to a group translating the Bible into another language. Do I really need to spend more time on social media or in front of the television tonight? What if instead of doing that, I open my Bible and spend time praying for a few groups in Central Asia that have no access to the gospel?

If you *are* called to focus your life on crossing cultural bound-
aries for the sake of the gospel, you will also have to make difficult
decisions. You might have to choose between living close to family
or following your call and moving halfway around the world. You
might have to tell your unbelieving parents that you've decided to
take their grandchildren to a place considered "unsafe." You might
need to give up modern conveniences like hot water and air condi-
tioning. You might live in a place where you are stared at, laughed
at, and often misunderstood.

As we saw in the first chapter, making these kinds of sacrifices
is part and parcel of being a disciple of Jesus Christ. It is for this
reason that Jesus told his disciples, "If anyone would come after
me, let him deny himself and take up his cross daily and follow
me" (Luke 9:23). A true disciple runs hard after Jesus because he
loves Jesus more than everything this world can offer. A true disciple is willing to give up the comforts and pleasures of this world
because he has already gained that which is most valuable.

After leaving that temple in early 2001, I knew that my life
would never be the same, but I never imagined how much sacrifice
would be required in the process. In the months after I returned
to the United States from Taiwan I realized that God was calling
me to move overseas. I also realized that the girl I was dating at the
time did not share my calling.

We had been dating for several years and had even discussed
marriage. Most of our friends assumed that we would get engaged
soon—either before or shortly after I graduated. But then I went
on that trip and I went in that temple and I saw the lostness of
the world around me. I began thinking more and more about that
question I just mentioned: "How can I continue to live in the same
way I did before?" God had burdened me for the people in the
world who have no access to the gospel. I wanted to spend my
life figuring out how to get the gospel to those peoples. And for
whatever reason, the girl I was dating—the girl I was supposed to
become engaged to soon—did not share that same burden.

Like the others in this book, I had to make a decision. In those
months after that trip, I began realizing that I could not embrace

my calling and share life with someone who did not have the same calling. The two were mutually exclusive. In the end I made the decision to break it off with the girl and move toward what God was calling me to.

Writing that sentence makes it all seem so easy, but at the time it certainly wasn't easy or comfortable. Not many people understood why I made this decision or any of the other strange decisions that my calling required. "Why give up such a nice job" some later asked me, "to move halfway around the world to a place where you don't have a job and don't know anyone?" Like the others in this book, I struggled with whether or not I was making the right decisions. What I did know was that I was bothered by the fact that so many people in the world didn't have access to the gospel. I was excited about the idea of going to those people, learning their language, and communicating the gospel with them. Moreover, because of God's calling, I was willing to sacrifice the aspects of my life that didn't conform to that calling.

I became interested in the topic of this book when I learned that others in church history had made similar decisions. At the time in my life when I was just figuring out what it meant to be called to missions, I thought I was the only one who had ever walked through these kinds of difficulties. One of the main points of this book, then, is to encourage you. If you are called to missions and are having to make some difficult decisions, know that you are not alone. You are not the first, nor are you the last to have to make sacrifices to obey your calling.

At the same time, we have to be careful. We don't want to assume that everyone's story will look the same. In my own life, while I was still processing my own calling, one of the people who had a tremendous impact on me was a senior adult named Mrs. Colson. She felt called to missions in her youth but later married someone who didn't share her calling. She and her husband faithfully served the church for many years and then in their retirement, her husband became ill and passed away. Though already in her seventies, Mrs. Colson began to go on short-term mission trips, started developing relationships with internationals who lived in her city, and even moved overseas for two years. Before she herself passed away in 2012, I did not know anyone more active or faithful in sharing the gospel cross-culturally.

Her story and my story look different. The goal is not that all of our testimonies will look the same but that we would all be faithful in obeying the Great Commission. How we do so will be different for each one of us. With that in mind, here are five principles that can help guide us toward greater Great Commission obedience.

First, whether or not you are called to cross-cultural missions, you *are* commanded to make disciples of all nations. Obeying the Great Commission doesn't mean that you need to sell all your belongings and move to Africa. It does mean that you will pray for people in other parts of the world to come to the knowledge of Christ. It does mean that you will give faithfully to support those who are involved in the frontline communication of the gospel with peoples of other ethnicities. And it does mean that you will be intentional in sharing the gospel with people around you, both those of similar cultural backgrounds and different ones. All of these activities will require sacrifice.

Second, if you are called to cross-cultural missions, you will have to make significant sacrifices. Obeying God's call on your life might require you to move somewhere far away from family. Like Hudson Taylor, it could be years until you see your parents and other family members again. Like Lottie Moon, you might be stared at and considered a "foreign devil" by many people. Like Henry Martyn, the climate, pollution, or water could make you ill. And like all three you will have difficulties understanding the local language and culture.

A third principle is if you are not married but think you might be one day, it is best to marry someone with the same calling. In 1 Corinthians 7, Paul provides some teaching on marriage and he states that in his opinion it is best to remain single. He recognizes, though, that not every one can accept that calling and states, "But if they cannot exercise self-control, they should marry. For it is better to marry than to burn with passion" (7:8). Paul understood that certain people did not have the gift of singleness and would desire the lifelong companionship that comes with marriage.

Paul's point, though, is not that these believers can marry anyone. They still need to evaluate whether marriage to a specific person is beneficial for them. It is for this reason that in a later letter to that church, Paul wrote, "Do not be unequally yoked with unbelievers" (2 Cor 6:14). Paul did not intend this command to be applied only to marriage, but it nonetheless does apply to marriage. And it doesn't only apply to whether or not believers should marry unbelievers. His point here is that if believers are "yoked" with unbelievers, the result will be that the unbelievers will lead the believers into sin. The principle is that believers must not develop close relationships with those who will lead them away from being faithful to God.

So even when a believer is considering marrying another believer, he should evaluate whether or not marrying that person will enable him to be more faithful in living out their calling. If someone is called to missions, she should not consider marrying someone who is not. Doing so will only lessen her ability to fulfill her calling.

Fourth, and along the same lines, it is better to stay single than marry someone who doesn't share your calling. In Paul's teaching on marriage in 1 Corinthians 7, he wrote to those who were unmarried saying, "It is good for them to remain single, as I am" (7:6). In Paul's mind, believers should consider singleness as a gift from God. It is a gift that believers can harness for the spread of the gospel and the advance of God's kingdom.

Churches need to stop treating single people as if something is wrong with them. I recently had a conversation with a student of mine who is single, female, and serving the Lord faithfully in a place where there are few male believers. She told me that some leaders in her church approached her and told her that they had found a husband for her in another state. All she needed to know was that he was believer. When she responded that she couldn't be sure he shared her same calling, they told her, "You just need to have faith." Their statement is based on the assumption that any normal person would want to get married and as long as both people are believers, marriage should be encouraged. These assumptions, though, are flawed. Singleness is a gift and it should only be given up when marriage enables us to be more faithful and more holy.

Finally, if you are married, under no circumstances are you called to sacrifice your marriage in order to obey your calling. In 1 Corinthians 7, Paul speaks to the married that "the wife should not separate from her husband, and the husband should not divorce her wife" (7:10–11). He even goes on to add that if one spouse is a believer and the other isn't, the believing spouse should not consider divorce. The point here is that marriage is a gift from God. Once married, spouses should work together to encourage one another to greater faithfulness. If a wife's calling is different from her husband's, they should work together to find a compromise where they both can be obedient to what God is calling them to do.

A student of mine told me that a missionary spoke to her church. She told the church that God called her to Africa but he called her husband to Canada. Since they were called to two different places, they got divorced! What shocked my student the most, though, was that the members of the church responded to her testimony by saying, "She has such great faith!"

Let me be as clear as possible. It is never God's will for someone to get divorced so that he/she can be a missionary. Doing so is not sacrifice and it is not an act of faith. It is utter foolishness. God is not honored when believers get divorced. He is glorified, however, when couples get on their knees, seek God's will, and find ways to mutually embrace each other's callings. Doing so is not always easy, but it is necessary. It may be that for a time a husband or wife lays aside his or her calling and embraces the other spouse's. Or it may be that they find a middle ground where both can pursue their callings. Either way, they must stay together and find a way forward.

We need to be careful here because, to be honest, the church has not always handled this issue well. We have already seen that Hudson Taylor began requiring husband and wife to share the same calling because both needed to be willing to embrace the difficulties of life in China. Before Taylor was born, William Carey left for India. His wife was opposed to India but in the end, she gave in and went. She never felt called to the work and she never adjusted to the stresses of cross-cultural life. She eventually developed mental problems. God called David Livingstone to Africa, and his wife accompanied him on his first few journeys to the continent. After their children were born, though, she decided to stay in England to educate their children. They were separated for four years.

Neither situation is ideal. God is not honored when one spouse is forced to obey the other spouse's calling, esp. if doing so means moving to a foreign country. Neither is he honored when one spouse abandons the other for years at a time in pursuit of his calling. God has designed marriage for our good, and spouses must put to death their own desires to help each other pursue faithfulness and holiness.

As we consider these principles and as we continue to examine the concept of sacrifice and obedience to the Great Commission, all of us should evaluate how we can better leverage our lives to expand God's kingdom in this world. The three people we studied in this book are helpful reminders that while *we* might know God, billions of other people in this world do not. So when we consider God's will for our lives, when we think about how we should spend our time, and when we evaluate what career paths we are best suited for, we also must consider how these choices relate to God's global mission. In the first chapter we explained that God's mission is for all people to know him and have a relationship with him. As the Psalmist says, "All the nations you have made shall come and worship before you, O Lord, and shall glorify your name" (86:9). For us, then, instead of just asking, "Which career will I enjoy the most?" We should also consider the question, "Which career best enables me to advance God's kingdom?"

In other words, we must begin to consider the choices of our lives through the lens of God's global mission. Hudson Taylor often reminded people that obedience to the Great Commission is not optional. At a conference in Perth, Australia, he posed the question to his audience, "Before the next Perth Conference twelve million more, in China, will have passed forever beyond our reach. What are we doing to bring them the tidings of redeeming love?"[1] He then continued:

> The Lord Jesus commands us, commands us each one individually, "Go," He says, "Go into all the world and preach the gospel to every creature." Will you say to Him, "It is not convenient"? Will you tell Him that you are busy fishing, have bought a piece of land, purchased five yoke of oxen, married a wife, or for other reasons cannot obey? Will He accept such excuses? Have we forgotten that "we must all stand before the judgment seat of Christ," that every one may receive the things done in the body. Oh, remember, pray for, labor for the unevangelized millions of China, or you will sin against your own soul![2]

On another occasion in Scotland, he told the crowd, "It will not do to say that you have no special call to go to China. With these facts before you, you need rather to ascertain whether you have a special call to stay at home."[3] Lottie Moon, as well, lamented the lack of commitment from so many in her denomination, writing,

> I wonder how many of us really believe that "it is more blessed to give than to receive." A woman who accepts that statement of our Lord Jesus Christ as a fact, and not as "impractical idealism," will make giving a principle of her life. . . . How many there are among our women, alas! alas! who imagine that because "Jesus paid it all," they need pay nothing, forgetting that the prime object of their salvation was that they should follow in the footsteps of Jesus Christ in bringing back a lost world to God, and so aid in bringing the answer to the petition our Lord taught his disciples: "Thy kingdom come."[4]

1. Taylor, *China Inland Mission*, 8.
2. Taylor, *China Inland Mission*, 8–9.
3. Taylor, *China Inland Mission*, 8
4. Harper, *Send the Light*, 224–25.

Along the same lines, in considering the Great Commission, John Piper has said that three types of people exist: "goers, senders, and the disobedient."[5] God is calling some people to commit their lives to taking the gospel to the peoples and ethnicities in this world who have never had an opportunity to hear the name of Jesus. These are the Lottie Moons and Henry Martyns of our generation. At the same time, the sending of these Lottie Moons would not be possible without people at home—people who live "normal" lives with normal jobs but are just as committed to God's global mission. They pray and give with passion, and in today's world, they can even go for a short time during their vacation days. Other than these two options, the third option is just plain old disobedience. If you are not going or sending, you are not obeying the Great Commission.

Piper explains that in God's economy, no difference exists between goers and senders. Both are equally important and equally vital. He writes, "So whether you are a goer or a sender is a secondary issue. That your heart beats with God's in his pursuit of worshippers from every tribe and tongue and people and nation is the primary issue."[6]

So as we consider these ideas, we should reflect on what God is calling us to sacrifice in order to obey the Great Commission more faithfully. In the same way, as we consider the issues of marriage and singleness, we should ask the question: Am I leveraging my current singleness to advance God's kingdom? If at some point in our lives, we consider getting married, we can ask the same question. Does marriage to this person enable me to better advance God's kingdom?

LOVE LOST

For the three people we have examined in this book, there was a point in their lives where the answer to that question was "No."

5. Piper, *Holy Ambition*, 167–68.
6. Piper, *Holy Ambition*, 168.

Henry Martyn was in love with Lydia Grenfell. He longed to spend time with her, and he never gave up hope that one day she would join him in India. At the same time, though, he recognized that his life was short. His time on earth was limited. To him, the most important thing in life was obeying God's call. We can recall the statement he wrote in his journal when considering his future.

> I have not felt such heart-rending pain since I parted with Lydia in Cornwall. But the Lord brought me to consider the folly and wickedness of all this. I could not help saying, "Go, Hindus, go on in your misery, let Satan still reign over you; for he that was appointed to labor among you is consulting his ease." No, thought I, earth and hell shall never keep me back from my work.[7]

All things being equal, he would choose to be with Lydia. He was happy with her. He enjoyed her company. They had much to talk about and many common interests. All things, though, were not equal. Martyn recognized that millions of people in India and in the Muslim world were lost, without the gospel, and were headed to a Christless eternity in hell. He could not choose the comfortable life. He would choose the easy road. He chose the "heart-rending pain" of saying no to the one he loved. Why? Because he recognized that marriage to her would not enable him to advance God's kingdom in this world. Saying yes to her would mean saying no to India. And God has called him to India.

In her life, Lottie Moon had to make a similar decision. At least once in her life, and possibly twice, she had the opportunity to marry a seminary professor. She herself might have had the opportunity to teach at the university level, perhaps even at Harvard. Not only would she have had the companionship of someone who was her intellectual equal, she would have had all the privileges that came with her husband's status. This situation was one for which she was gifted, excited about, and equipped for. And yet, in the end she said, "No."

---

7. Sargent, *Life and Letters*, 86.

Why would she say no to such an opportunity for happiness and fulfillment? She said no because she could not say yes to this opportunity and say yes to God's call on her life. Being married to Toy would not enable her to obey God's call and advance his kingdom. She chose singleness over marriage. She labored on in China for another thirty years. Why? Because God's glory and the opportunity to tell others about Christ was more valuable to her than all the happiness the world could offer her. She embraced loneliness, hardships, separation from family, uncomfortable beds, dirty floors, lack of privacy, and food she didn't like. She embraced these things because with them came the opportunity to take the name of Christ to places where it had never before been heard. And for her, being a part of that endeavor was the greatest joy this world could offer.

Hudson Taylor had to answer this question several times and in several different ways. He was first in love with Marianne who asked him, "Must you go to China?" The ideal woman was in love with him, and they even became engaged. The perfect life beckoned him. He wrote in his journal during those days the questions that plagued him, "Is it all worthwhile? Why should you go to China? Why toil and suffer all your life for an ideal of duty? Give it up now, while you can yet win her."[8] The idea of China was just a childhood dream. Here was true happiness for the taking. And yet, as we saw, Hudson Taylor said no to this kind of happiness.

A second time he had to consider this question as he corresponded with Elizabeth Sissons. At that point he had already been in China long enough to know that missions in China would be filled with hardships and trials. He was desperately lonely. A civil war was raging around him. Plenty of reasons existed to justify his leaving China and marrying Elizabeth. No one in England would have questioned his zeal or piety if he had returned home then. In fact, he probably would have returned home to the sound of praise and people saying, "You did well in China!" and "We're proud of you for taking the gospel to those heathen!"

8. Taylor, *Early Years*, 123.

Taylor, though, didn't live for the praise of men. He really didn't care what others thought about him, including those who were on the field with him. He was driven by one thing and one thing only—proclaiming the gospel to the Chinese. So for the second time in his life he considered a potential wife and concluded that being married to her would not allow him to pursue his calling. Being married to her would not enable him to advance God's kingdom.

Eventually, though, Taylor met someone who shared his calling and he recognized that marriage to Maria helped to advance the gospel. Even then, though, the commitment to their calling and to life in China meant that they were sick for much of their adult lives. Several of their children died. At any point, Taylor could have made the decision to move back to England. It would have been easy to rationalize that decision given how sick and exhausted they were. He could have continued to lead the CIM from England. He could have mobilized and raised support for other missionaries while in England.

Living in England, though, was not his or Maria's calling. He was called to be in China and to lead the CIM from China. Doing so meant dealing with the relentless heat of summer and the fevers that often accompanied it. Obeying the call of God meant laying his life and the lives of his wife and children on the altar of Christ. Living in China and laboring for the salvation of the Chinese meant that he had to sacrifice the love of his life. He held her hand and watched her die, all the while knowing that a life of comfort and ease in England would have meant many more years together.

And these three are not alone in church or missions history. The annals of church history are filled with testimonies of those who valued the exaltation of Christ over against the pleasures and comforts of this world. We might also consider Jim Elliot, Nate Saint, Ed McCully, Roger Youderian, and Pete Fleming who were martyred in Ecuador as they attempted to take the gospel to a tribal group nicknamed "savages" because they speared to death all those who entered their land.[9] All five were in their late twenties and

---

9. Their story is recounted in Elliot, *Through Gates of Splendor*.

early thirties, married, and with young children. Like most people their age, though, they were not settling down and enjoying life. They were dreaming about how to get the gospel to peoples who had never heard the name of Jesus.

We might also consider the life of David Brainerd.[10] Highly educated, several God-ordained events forced him to give up further education, and in the process, he became burdened for the American Indians who had never heard the gospel. Like Henry Martyn, his health was not good. Nonetheless, he was willing to suffer if it meant that others might have access to the gospel. Eventually he developed tuberculosis and died at the age of twenty-nine. In the process he became friends with Jonathan Edwards, and it seems fell in love with Edwards' daughter Jerusha. While taking care of him in the final weeks of his life, Jerusha also contracted tuberculosis and died. For both of them, living out the gospel was more important than health and happiness.

YOUR STORY

And on and on we could continue with other examples from throughout church history. No shortage exists in church history of people who loved Christ more than life and limb. For all these, the kingdom was like the man in Matthew 13:44. For him the treasure in the field was more valuable than everything else he owned. For the three in this book and for so many others in church history, they considered the benefits and pleasures of this life and then compared them to the glory of God in the face of Jesus Christ. For them, the fading glory of this world paled in comparison with the matchless beauty of the gospel.

At this point, though, we might pause and consider your story. What will your story be? As you've read the testimonies of those in the book, how has God burdened you or awakened you? What sacrifices is he calling you to make for the sake of his kingdom? How does your career or current course of study intersect with

10. See Brainerd, *Life and Diary*; Piper, *David Brainerd*.

God's global mission? In what ways can you leverage your abilities and experience so that the people in the least reached parts of our world might finally have access to the gospel?

The three missionaries in this book sacrificed earthly love for the sake of the gospel. In the first chapter we saw that contemporary culture values finding that special someone. Many believe that if they just find the right person, life will be filled with happiness and fulfillment. We see these values personified in movies and echoed in pop songs. Scripture, though, gives us a different set of values. The Bible teaches that love for Christ and obedience to his commands should be the highest value of our lives. Is that true of your life? Would others look at your life and see that the most important aspect of your life is love for Christ and a desire to make him known?

Consider the world around us. In early 2018, the world population is more than 7 billion.[11] For years, missiologists have discussed the concept of unreached people groups (UPGs). These UPGs are less than 2 percent Christian and have little to no access to the gospel. Of the world's 7 billion people, more than 3 billion are part of an UPG. That means that an estimated 42 percent of all the people who are alive today live amongst a people with little to no access to the gospel.

In more recent years, mission organizations have monitored unengaged UPGs or UUPGs. Like UPGs, a UUPG is also less than 2 percent Christian and has little to no access to the gospel. Moreover, it is considered unengaged because currently no known missionaries are working to make the gospel known to that people. So for these groups, not only have they not heard of the name of Jesus Christ, no one is even actively working to see that the gospel is proclaimed to them. These ethnicities have no hope of hearing the gospel any time soon. One organization estimates that in Northern Africa and the Middle East as much as 17.4 percent of the population is UUPGs.[12]

11. See the Joshua Project's "Global Realities."
12. See the International Mission Board's "People and Places."

And to speak of UPGs and UUPGs is really only the tip of the iceberg when it comes to the missionary task of the church. Space limits us from delving into what it might take to make the gospel known to any one of these groups. We haven't even mentioned the mega cities of the world, where tens of millions of people live in close proximity. These massive population segments are often filled with many different people groups, intermingling and over-lapping in huge urban sprawls. We must also recognize that in many parts of the world some people have been evangelized but never really discipled. Huge needs exist in these parts of the world for the church and for the lost.

The church's mission certainly does not belong to the church in the West alone. For the three people examined in this book, it was the church in America and England that sent them to some other part of the world. For much of the last two hundred years, the church's understanding of missions has been shaped by that paradigm—the church in the West sends missionaries to other part of the world. More and more, though, it is believers in Asia, Africa, and Latin American who are setting the standard in mis-sions. Believers from these parts of the world are much more willing to suffer and to sacrifice earthly pleasures for the sake of advancing the gospel.

What about us? What will our story be? Seeing the state of the world around us, understanding the great gospel needs, rec-ognizing that millions in our world have no access to saving faith in Jesus Christ, will we continue to live in the same way we did before? In this book we have studied the lives of three people who, when faced with the reality around them, could no longer go on living in the same way they had before. They were willing to sac-rifice earthly pleasures, even love itself, to see that others in their world—those they had never even met—might have an opportu-nity to hear the gospel in their lifetime. They lived for one thing. That one thing was more precious and more valuable than all this world could offer them. And that one thing was simple—to know Christ and to make him known.

QUESTIONS FOR CONSIDERATION

1. How would you describe God's will for your life? Do you feel called to missions?

2. What kind of sacrifices is God calling you to make for his kingdom?

3. How do the five principles recounted in this chapter help you to understand the kind of sacrifices you need to be making? Which principle best speaks to your current situation?

4. How does the Great Commission and the knowledge of God's global mission to make himself known affect all our choices and decisions?

5. As you've read this book, how have the stories of these missionaries affected you and how you view God's call on your life? How have their sacrifices influenced how you understand obedience to God?

6. How will you live differently in light of the state of lostness in the world today?

Bibliography

Akin, Danny. "A Word From Paul For A Southern Baptist Convention Great Commission Resurgence Advance For The 21st Century." http://www.danielakin.com/wp-content/uploads/2009/06/romans-1514-23-a-word-from-paul-for-a-southern-baptist-convention-great-commission-resurgence-manuscript-ds.pdf.

Allen, Catherine B. *The New Lottie Moon Story*. Nashville: Broadman, 1980.

Barclay, James. *Jerusalem As It Was, As It Is, and As It Is To Be*. Philadelphia: Desilver, 1859.

Brainerd, David. *The Life and Diary of David Brainerd with Notes and Reflections by Jonathan Edwards*. Edited by Jonathan Edwards. Reprint. Chicago: Moody, 1970.

Broomhall, A. J. *The Shaping of Modern China: Hudson Taylor's Life and Legacy*. 2 vols. Pasadena: William Carey Library, 2005.

Cromarty, Jim. *For the Love of India: The Story of Henry Martyn*. Webster, NY: Evangelical, 2005.

Elliot, Elizabeth. *Through Gates of Splendor*. Rev. ed. Carol Stream, IL: Tyndale, 1981.

Harper, Keith, ed. *Send the Light: Lottie Moon's Letters and Other Writings*. Atlanta: Mercer University Press, 2002.

International Mission Board. "People and Places." https://www.imb.org/people-and-places/.

Joshua Project. "Global Statistics." https://joshuaproject.net/people_groups/statistics.

Lawrence, Una Roberts. *Lottie Moon*. Nashville: Sunday School Board of the Southern Baptist Convention, 1927.

Piper, John. *David Brainerd: May I Never Loiter on My Heavenly Journey*. Minneapolis: Desiring God, 2012.

————. *A Holy Ambition: To Preach Where Christ Has Not Been Named*. Minneapolis: Desiring God, 2011.

Pollock, John. *Hudson Taylor & Maria: A Match Made in Heaven*. Ross-shire, Scotland: Christian Focus, 1996.

Bibliography

Rhea, Sarah J. *Life of Henry Martyn, Missionary to India and Persia, 1781 to 1812*. Missionary Annals Series. Chicago: Woman's Presbyterian Board of Foreign Missions of the Northwest, 1888.

Riley, Rachel. "What Are the Odds of Love? Rachel Riley Reveals All." https://www.eharmony.co.uk/dating-advice/dating/odds-of-love#. WymDoFMvzOQ.

Sargent, John. *The Life and Letters of Henry Martyn*. Carlisle, PA: Banner of Truth, 1985.

Smith, George. *Henry Martyn: Saint and Scholar, First Modern Missionary to the Mohammedans, 1781–1812*. London: Religious Tract Society, 1892. Kindle edition.

Sullivan, Regina D. *Lottie Moon: A Southern Baptist Missionary to China in History and Legend*. Southern Biography Series, edited by Andrew Burstein. Baton Rouge: Louisiana State University Press, 2011.

Taylor, Howard. *Hudson Taylor and the China Inland Mission: The Growth of a Work of God*. Classic Reprint Series. London: Forgotten Books, 2015.

———. *Hudson Taylor in Early Years: The Growth of a Soul*. London: China Inland Mission, 1958.

———. *Hudson Taylor's Spiritual Secret*. Chicago: Moody Bible Institute, 1932.

Taylor, J. Hudson. *China's Spiritual Need and Claims*. 7th ed. London: Morgan & Scott, 1887.

www.ingramcontent.com/pod-product-compliance
Lightning Source LLC
Chambersburg PA
CBHW070505090426

42735CB00012B/2678